Robert Levithan

THE NEW 60

OUTLIVING YOURSELF AND REINVENTING A FUTURE

Introduction by Mark Matousek,
Author of *Ethical Wisdom*

Forward by Tracey Jackson
Author of *Between A Rock And A Hot Place*

ISBN-10: 1468009893
ISBN-13: 9781468009897

Library of Congress Control Number: 2011961920
CreateSpace, North Charleston, SC

Photo by C. Harrison

"The quality of life is not determined by the circumstances."
Sally Fisher

" The good die young, we live forever..."
Levithan Family Motto

To my brothers and sisters who did not survive AIDS —
And to those of us who did.

And for Lou and Alice with luck and love...

CONTENTS

FORWARD

Robert Levithan writes with the wisdom of a sage, the enthusiasm of a kid, the depth of someone who has seen the world from all sides and the humor of someone who always knows where the joke is hiding.

While he is often classified as a gay writer, or writer of subjects pertaining to the gay experience, he manages to take all of his topics and somehow turn them into universal stories. I have never read one of Robert's pieces and not walked away with a great life lesson. In all of his work one sees oneself, one's friends, one's lovers, and one's life.

He is sometimes the benevolent father, sometimes the naughty, yet learned instructor, often the whimsical brother or sister you wish you had and he can even be the gossipy neighbor upstairs. But while he is able to pull off all these various personas he is always, without hesitation, or question dealing up heavy doses of the truth; his own and thus ours. For me that is what makes him not only a wonderful writer, but a writer who transcends race, gender, and sexual identity. He writes about the human condition in all its various incarnations and while forcing us to think, he ultimately always reminds us how lucky we are to be alive and to relish every thing that comes our way.

— Tracey Jackson, Screenwriter
Author of *Between A Rock and a Hot Place*,
and blogger.

PREFACE

I have always been ambivalent about ambition. A part of me has wanted to shine in the world, to be acknowledged and seen. Another part of me has longed for the luxury of quiet, and time for simpler, quotidian pleasures: lingering over coffee and the crossword in the morning, long walks on the beach with my dog, hours in bed with a delicious novel or memoir, dinners at home or out with lovers and friends, extended travels to exotic places....

When I semi-retired to Santa Fe in the very late '80s, I was facing a likely young death from AIDS and I found myself living a version of that quieter life. I also found that being of service was essential to my serenity, so I helped organize HIV and grief support groups, which I facilitated. I began to take courses that eventually led to a master's degree in Transformational Counseling, and I began to write about my experience of facing mortality as part of a writing group.

I outlived myself and I arrived back in my native New York City in 1995 to reinvent a future that now includes an active career as a psychotherapist and workshop leader, and as a columnist and writer.

The New 60 is an edited version of thirty-three columns that I wrote as an exploration of approaching (and, eventually, arriving at) 60—an age that had once seemed beyond my reach.

This is that journey—much of it a surprise even to me.

Robert Levithan

January 4, 2012

ACKNOWLEDGEMENTS

To Christo Harrison, I owe the inspiration—brainstorming by the Hudson one August day—and for a large measure of confidence in my voice.

Amy Gross has been a solid guide, mentor and editor—trusted and swift, generous beyond reason.

Mark Matousek, the man and the writer, has inspired me along the way and his introduction honors and humbles—thank you my brother from a different mother.

Tracey Jackson is an amazing force. I love having her energy with me!

Robin Maltz is a delight to work with and a crack editorial eye.

I would like to thank Jon Barrett for immediately saying yes when I approached him at the The Advocate, and Ross Von Metzke for stewarding the birth of The New 60 on Advocate.com. The Good

Men Project gives it a second and ever so worthy home, and The Huffington Post lets me reach an even broader audience.

Certain agents and editors gave me early and needed encouragement by turning me down with praise and grace—an art.

I am inspired by my family, especially David, the writer, Sarah, my friend, and my brother Jack who has commented on every post and column with such generosity and insight. And my other families: The Freibergs, The Carlins, The Solomons.

The Brunch Club (Andrea, Sara, Christopher, and Babak) provided material and laughter; Jerry Chasen. solid advice; and Crayton Robey, strength. Thanks to Florence Falk for grace and Cy O'Neal for early support, and to Billy Merrill for helping his friend's uncle!

Karen Fuchs shines as a warrior and for capturing Sophie and me with her exquisite eye!

Writing together has kept me together: Thank you to Sally Fisher and Carol Morgan for all of our sessions over the past 15 years—and to Joan Logghe and the Santa Fe AIDS writing group where I was able to write myself a future.

Finally, my gratitude to my clients, the Friends In Deed community, The Mastery Workshop community--all of the inspiring men and women who have trusted me with their stories.

It took a village! If I missed anyone, please know that your contribution was so seamless that I might not have noted it, but the fabric knows...

INTRODUCTION

One blistering summer day in 1991, Robert Levithan and I were having the biggest fight of our 30-year friendship next to a lake in Abiqui, New Mexico. We were locking horns over sex, again, and what began as a genteel chat about monogamy (my preference) versus the right to improvisational erotic freedom (his domain) had exploded into a screaming match on the beach. Never before or after have we yelled at one another.

"Love is not a cage!" Robert bellowed. I'd never seen him so furious before. Robert prides himself on being judicious, seeing both sides, embracing difference, eschewing violence. He is the least judgmental person I know and among the most generous minded. Yet here he was having a hissy fit, red-faced, clenched-fisted, hugely pissed off, offended by my pious superiority. "We have the right to choose what we want for *ourselves!*" Robert said.

"You need to grow up. Trust is more important than sex," I told him.

"How can you trust somebody who's lying to you? Or who *you're* lying to?"

"Who's lying?" I asked him.

"*You* are." Robert stared me down. "If you think that everyone wants the same thing."

"Everyone wants to be loved," I said.

Both of us were right, of course. Finally, we agreed to disagree. I called him an insatiable fantasist. He thought I was rigid and scared. We've been disagreeing over sex and love ever since, but what strikes me most at this moment, with *The New 60* manuscript on my desk, is how deeply the seeds of this book had been planted in him decades before he actually sat down to write. The themes that obsess him have not wavered. He believes in the supremacy of personal choice, in *joie de vivre* at all costs, open-mindedness to a potential fault, and the refusal to play by oppressive rules. He cares about imagination and surprise (especially in the art of living), paternal worry over people he loves, devotion to beauty (over things like money, convention, obedience) in its myriad forms -- from his world-class collection of photographs (many of Robert himself posed in his former, Teutonic glory for artists including Robert Mapplethorpe, Peter Hujar, and Duane Michals) to a windy beach in Sagaponack -- free thinking and experimentation, dependability, and not being bored. He is moved by the sacredness of white spaces and by family unity, beginning with his own illustrious clan, and extending to a global swarm of lifelong friends. Most of all, Robert believes in gratitude for the time we are here and in *self-reinvention* most of all, the faith to keep growing against the odds and the will to construct the most splendid, original life that each of us possibly can.

That passion informs the essays in this book. Having known the author in most of the ways two men can know each other – as partners, roommates, confidantes, best friends, PWAs, dharma brothers, and travel companions – I can tell you with certainty that he walks the talk of the wisdom he shares. At a stage when lots of us are already protecting our lives in mothballs, terrified to change direction, Robert views himself as a work in progress (like Disneyland, he will never be finished.) To criticism that he should act his age, Robert reminds people that he never expected to see 60, which leaves him free to make it up for himself. I'll never forget walking into a hospital room in Santa Fe and finding him with an oxygen mask over his face, his eyes filled with fear; or how different he was after he nearly died. The pre-AIDS Robert was more of a pleaser; he cared about being the good boy, keeping up appearances, being politically correct, and not ruffling feathers. Today, he cares more about telling the truth than he does about being a poster boy for squeaky clean. This is the mark of a post-catastrophe person. To those friends who would like him to be more modest, Robert responds by reminding them (not so gently sometimes) that it's his life. To those who warn him to be more chaste (as a single man and hexagenarian), he answers with a memoirist's *cri de coeur* – if you've got it, why not flaunt it? -- and goes on writing exactly what he wants.

I'm glad that he does and you should be, too. Confessional, wise, and experience-based, the essays in *The New 60* address many thorny, fascinating issues. Ageism, homophobia, anti-Semitism, self-loathing, dating, commitment, and yes, sex in its many, confounding forms, and how to reconcile erotic desire with love – are explored in intimate, heartfelt detail. He writes about death, love, commitment, friendship, hypocrisy, and the strange allure of his ubiquitous Segway. Mostly, he writes about how to live better, more hungrily and truthfully, more passionately, and ethically, during our brief, precious lives. He's fought long and hard to get where he is – even though Robert likes to make it look easy – and *The New 60* is the fruit of all that labor. I still disagree with him on certain topics, but I never doubt his sincerity. I never doubt the depth of his soul, how much he cares, how truly he loves, or the lengths he will go to tell the truth. He has opened my eyes and sometimes shamed me for the narrowness of my own heart. For this, I am eternally grateful. Ever since that day in Abiqui, and our Antonioni-meets-Almodovar fight on the beach, I've known that my friend was a fighter. Now, he's become a teacher, too. Your eyes will be opened by reading this book.

Mark Matousek, author of *Ethical Wisdom*

THE NEW 60

A year from now I will be 60. Holy shit! How did this happen? I remember my 70-year-old mother looking in the mirror and saying, "Who is that old woman? I'm 17!"

When I was 40, I never expected to see 60, certainly not as the vital and healthy man I am today. I tested positive for HIV as part of a study in 1984. My immune system crashed in 1994. I won a lottery to receive compassionate-usage access to a workable cocktail in 1995. My immune system began to rebuild then, and I am blessed to be in extraordinary health today. When I turned 50, I realized that I had no vision for my 50s: I had been in survival mode since I was 35.

At my 50th birthday party, a friend said, "Welcome to your 50s ... it's when you can stop caring what anyone thinks." That has been the fuel for this decade's exploration: What if I am fully me and don't give a fuck what others think? One of my first choices was to go back to calling myself Bobby. The kid in me is definitely Bobby. Robert is the 50-something adult and an appropriate professional name.

I am fortunate: I am 6 feet 1 inch tall. I weigh 172 pounds. I have a full head of hair. I have been 17 and 35 simultaneously — a kid and a level-headed adult. My physical image of myself is 35. When it comes to sex, I'm 17. My number 1 boyfriend (I have not been in a traditional monogamous relationship for a number of years) says that it's a good thing I am so goofy or people would hate me.

Most of us have an inner age. I've asked hundreds of clients and friends, "How old are you inside?" The answer is usually 16 or 17, sometimes older ... once, it was 9.

I do serious work in the world as a group facilitator at Friends in Deed in New York City, as a leader of the Mastery Workshop nationwide, and in private practice as a psychotherapist, primarily working with life-changing crisis and transition. However serious my work is, I try not to take myself at all seriously.

I do believe in reinvention — of the individual and of the roles each of us play in our personal and public lives. Approaching 60 inspires me to reflect on many issues, including my vanity, my health, and my own ageism, especially the internalized prejudices about being this age, as a man, a gay man, a white man, an American, as someone who tested positive for HIV in 1984.

My number 1 boyfriend also says that I am "shameless." That is the triumph of my 50s (based on hard work in my 30s and 40s). Now I am applying that freedom to a vision for my next decade. Along the way, I'll be letting go of baggage and dealing with fears and ultimately, once again, I will be challenged to embrace the courageous, shameless Bobby/ Robert who is ready for his sensational 60s.

My noisy life has been extraordinary in so many ways. My ambition is to explore 60 as an exciting threshold and to bust my own internalized ageism as a window into our unnecessarily ageist culture.

IN DOG YEARS

I live with an overeducated bitch.

Sophie is beautiful. She's an elegant blond with a bit of Grace Kelly hauteur. She has shared my bed for almost five years. She has the equivalent of a Ph.D. She is often photographed and has appeared in Oprah's magazine, *O At Home,* on the Web, and in newspaper features. She assists with more than 100 clients a week. She is intelligent. She is good at getting her way. She hates to be left home alone.

By the way, she's a yellow Labrador.

Sophie was a guide dog for the blind, decommissioned at three years of age for "not wanting to work." She's just too social to be a seeing-eye dog. When she first came to live with me, I called her "The Stepford Dog" because she was too good to be real. As the years go by, she becomes less perfect and more of an individual, stubborn and wily, and therefore even more lovable in my estimation.

Sophie is not my first dog. Knickerbocker was also a yellow Lab, rescued from the Santa Fe Animal Shelter at about two years of age. He was handsome and dignified, joining me as I turned 40. At that point in my life, I had real concerns about his outliving me. My will provided a fund for Knick and stated who was to get him in the event of my death (presumably from AIDS). He died in 2000. I am still here. Of course, Sophie might outlive me, but I now live with the expectation that I will see her age and die, that once again my heart will be broken and once again I will go on.

Everything in my life is predicated on different assumptions and possibilities than it was fifteen or twenty years ago. As I approach 60, Sophie and I will peak at the same age and then, if nature takes its course, she will age more rapidly than I will. This is amazing to me. Still.

Outliving yourself brings with it so many gifts and certain challenges, such as outliving my father and my dogs, some of my friends and also, outliving my firm skin and springy knees. I'm not complaining. I'm observing it. I am savoring it.

My friend Wayde realized the other day that he is now the same age his father was at his death. He says every moment from now on he will, in a sense, have outlived his father's experience of life. Wayde is only 32. My father was almost 94 when he died, so I may or may not have the experience of outliving my father, but I live in it as a possibility. After all, my family's motto is "The Good Die Young. We Live Forever."

NEWLY SINGLE

I'm turning 60 and officially single. In our culture this is considered somewhat tragic. We are so couple-centric and ageist that to not have a partner after 40 is often seen as a kind of failure. I don't buy it.

Many of my clients struggle with this. Yesterday, a 60-ish client talked about his hesitation at ending a toxic relationship for fear of being alone for the rest of his life. We talked about solitude versus loneliness, and about balancing solitude with relationships, romantic and otherwise. It's important to be at home in oneself. I always tell my clients that a healthy relationship has "two I's and a we." We should all be working on our healthy "I." To create and nurture a "we" is both challenging and enlivening.

I do want a partner.

In the song "Being Alive," composer-lyricist Stephen Sondheim writes, "Somebody hold me too close / Somebody hurt me too deep / Somebody sit in my chair / Ruin my sleep / And make me alive ... " He speaks of not really having a relationship until he was 60. I like hearing that there is time for another great love.

My last relationship, with C., was a success. We are both better, stronger, more realized than when we met almost six years ago. We were always honest and respectful and told our truth as fast as we knew it, and we remain "exes with benefits." However, we let go of plans for a joint future a few months ago. My first long-term lover has been like a brother for over twenty-five years, and A., the man who took my virginity in Italy almost forty years ago, is my friend and current landlord.

Why not?

Forms change. I don't stop loving.

My dear departed friend Felicity Mason wrote a memoir called *The Love Habit* when she was my age, all about her liaisons with young men: "I don't subtract, I only add," she would say.

I remember being at tea in her apartment on Central Park West, a gathering which included both of her ex-husbands, one with his third wife; Felicity's long-term ex-lover and his male lover; and the boy from the copy shop she was shtupping at the time. Felicity is one of my role models.

The other night I was strolling back from an early dinner with a romantic friend when out of nowhere, he said, "You're still in love with C., aren't you?" At first I demurred. Then it became clear. "Yes, I'm still in love with him. I'm still in love with M. and A. and you!"

Forms change. I don't stop loving.

When my father died, C. was there to hold my hand and walk with me behind the casket, to shovel dirt on the coffin. M. was there as well. To paraphrase Freud: Life as we know it is just too too difficult to go it alone. Does that mean we need a partner? I'd like one, and I know that on my own I am whole — and surrounded by support. And I miss being someone's number one. I miss having that special someone whom I call first when I get big news of any kind. I made an offer on a loft last week; C. was out of town, and I felt painfully singular. M. kindly came over and saw the space, but somehow I missed the sharing of it as "we."

For now, I am a single man, almost 60.

Some men find my life crowded. They want more emotional exclusivity. A man I dated recently said he felt the presence of my exes. I felt the lack of his. To me, it's a bad sign when all of the ex-boyfriends are assholes. That would make me just the next asshole-in-waiting.

We'll see who's up for the next part of the journey — and my baggage: a full rich life that includes an overeducated Labrador and some wonderful exes.

Is it unrealistic to see the heart as continually able to expand? I hope not.

SIXTY WITH A SIX PACK?

Recently I looked at a picture of myself at 37. I remember being so concerned about aging then, even though I look great and so young. Twenty years from now (or even ten), I will probably look at a picture of myself today and think I look great and young. It would be a shame to miss enjoying what I have now or to have it only in retrospect.

To age gracefully, we need to balance health and vanity. I am propelled by both to take care of myself, and I have had opportunities to explore my attachment to both as well.

Back in 1994, after two weeks in bed with serious AIDS-related pneumonia, I had not "lost my looks," but I had lost my body. The flesh hung on my thighs. My body had less muscle tone than my energetic 84-year-old father's. I was tired after walking across my small walled garden in Santa Fe.

I decided to see what I could do about it. I remember doing three push-ups one day, twelve leg lifts the next day, and building incrementally until about a year later I was at the gym when a man approached me and said, "You look like you are in good shape and might be able to give me help with this machine." Only then did I realize that I had fully brought back my body.

A few months ago I saw a dance performance titled GIMP. The choreographer was working with several "other-bodied" dancers and two or three dancers from her regular company. It was startling to actually be invited to watch a one-armed woman dance a sexy duet with a man with cerebral palsy, a gorgeous woman with one hand, among others. In one section they spoke about being looked at, challenging us to stare, about proudly being their beautiful, different selves. For me, the most confrontational dancer was a man from her company who, to me, looked to have HIV-related lipodystrophy, visible signs of illness, or medication side effects. He was who I might have become; who I might still become.

In the car riding home, I turned to my boyfriend, both of us brought to tears by the exquisite courage and odd beauty we had just witnessed, and wondered aloud, "I forget to be grateful for my body ... I am obsessing about having a six-pack when I turn 60. Perhaps I've lost perspective."

Now, as I enter my 60th year, I am nearly giddy at the state of my health, my strength, and my vitality. I have challenges: My knees hurt walking up the stairs, one shoulder rotates only partially, and in order to function, I consider Advil almost as important as the antivirals and vitamins that sustain my immune system and the hormone replacement therapy that contributes to my energy level. In sum, I am a successful holistic science project — reaping the benefits of good genes, good medicine, a healthy lifestyle, and discipline.

I enjoy my body, and it is a challenge to reconcile my vanity with my desire to be fine with any circumstance. When I was so ill, I was surprisingly peaceful. I knew in my gut that I was not just my body. Along with my health, my vanity returned, tempered by an experience of loss that had turned out to be temporary. Certainly, the future will include loss of energy, further loss of skin texture, and more lines in my already craggy face.

Accepting the aging process is key. A little vanity pushes us to care for ourselves. A lot of vanity usually takes away enjoyment of who we are at our core. This is a practice for most of us, considering the pressure to be "young" in our culture. I pray that I can embrace this process and enjoy what I have at each stage fully, and move on with some measure of grace.

WHY WE LIE ABOUT AGE

"If people knew my real age, I'd never work again." I have heard this plaint more than once. The last time was the day before yesterday, when talking about age with a vivacious, successful Brazilian friend. She doesn't dare tell the truth about her age.

Why do most people lie about their age? Because they think they have to. Our culture at large — and our gay male culture specifically — embody ageism. Young is good. Older is less good.

On Facebook few people put their year of birth. For online dating sites, not to mention hookup sites, there is such pressure to lie that those of us who tell the truth are odd men out. When I post my age as 59, men think I'm somewhere between 64 and 75. Again, why do we lie about our age?

Ageism, yes. Internalized ageism, as well. Internalized prejudice is when we operate out of a learned prejudice about something we are: I have been exploring my own internalized homophobia, anti-Semitism, and AIDS-phobia, however subtle or overt, for years. I lead workshops where we have looked at our internalized prejudice, such as racism, classism, and genderism.

How do we know when we are operating from internalized prejudice?: When we try to "pass" without cause. When we are living in the belief that what we are is less than what other people are; when we have bought into other people's prejudices (which do exist) and perceive danger even when it doesn't exist.

There are situations where honesty about my sexual orientation, my HIV status, or my religious heritage could get me killed. I would lie or hide if my life were at stake. However, often I observe "passing" behavior when there is no danger. Most of us will not suffer harm if we are honest about our sexuality or our age. We do, however, suffer psychically, from constant denial of the truth about who or what we.

In the workshops there is one internalized prejudice that absolutely everyone relates to: internalized ageism. When asked, all perceived the statement "You look younger than your age" as a compliment. We are passing. At 90, my father would be insulted if someone didn't say he looked at least 15 years younger.

Recently, I dated a man I met online. His profile said 38. I didn't doubt it. In conversation, it came up that he is actually 47. I asked him why he lied. "Because I look 38," he said. He didn't like it when I suggested that he is perpetuating distorted behaviors around age. To paraphrase Gloria Steinem, "this is what 47 looks like."

We are complicit if we continue to play this game. I received a comment that an online photo of mine "had been royally airbrushed."

This is not true. And it reflects a too-oft accepted idea of what a 59-year-old man looks like. Age is how long we have been in this body — it is not our vitality, it is not our beauty.

My friend David heard I was writing about why people lie about their age: In his best Olympia-Dukakis-in-Moonstruck voice, he quipped, "Because they are afraid of death." My response is that we are afraid of perceived social death. We act as if we might die, but we don't.

Telling the truth about our age could be neutral. The more of us who do it, the more of a norm it will become.

I AM WHO I AM

I am a privileged man. I have not suffered for being completely out about my sexuality or my HIV status. Sometimes I forget how rare that makes me.

Something is missing from the picture: my full civil rights. I was not initially a big proponent of gay marriage. I was content with the idea of civil union status. My generation had been brainwashed that we were less than, so I was willing to accept less in order to keep the peace. My heart changed when my nephew, David Levithan, the Lambda award-winning author of *Boy Meets Boy*, wrote that he wouldn't accept civil unions or a lesser status than marriage because he would not accept it if they said Jews could only have civil unions.

Right: I do not accept second-tier status for people of color, or women, so why would I accept it for myself. I want every right that comes with being an American citizen.

A dear friend read some of my writing while in Malawi where she is working on a microeconomics project for local women, the very day I read that Malawi had arrested and convicted a gay male couple for "gross indecency" for celebrating their engagement. I asked my friend if she was aware of this. Her prompt reply, "It's despicable." Of course, any friend of mine would condemn discrimination against homosexuals. And I am relieved that after the international outcry, the president of Malawi pardoned the young men. And yet my heart is not easy. This is outrageous.

Where does my outrage live? I am amazed that I can sleep at night. And I do. Compartmentalization may be necessary to function in this world. However, we must stay awake, we must take action, we must recognize that silence equals complicity.

In private practice and at Friends in Deed, I encourage a focus on living in the present, on taking actions which support our health, well-being, and integrity. I am not in favor of martyrdom, as it is not functional. I do, therefore, believe in service, in taking care of yourself so that you can take care of others. Our human rights and the rights of our sisters and brothers are an integral part of our lives. This is not a luxury issue. It is part of self-care.

Last night I saw the brilliant revival of *La Cage aux Folles* on Broadway. What was cutting-edge twenty-five years ago is still powerful and, sadly, timely. When Albin sang "I Am What I Am," my tears were both historic and current.

I often write about internalized prejudice. I want young gay men and women to grow up expecting their civil rights. I look forward to it being taken for granted by younger generations the way that young people of color know that discrimination against them is illegal. I want to be happily stunned like the older black people I know who never thought they'd see a black president in their lifetime — by seeing a gay president in mine!

How is it that I am living in the 21st century in what was once the most progressive nation on earth, and I do not have my full civil rights? This is as outrageous as what is happening in Malawi and elsewhere because of the context. My grandparents were all born in Europe and chose to come to the United States in order to escape oppression. As their heir, I choose not to be complacent.

I am committed to having full legal rights before I leave this body. I am about to be 60 and therefore could have a decade or two to enjoy them as well.

I am what I am, and I deserve to live and die a free man.

MIND GAMES

One day a few years ago, I was sitting in a bath, and suddenly realized that the only thing standing between me and relaxation and pleasure ... was me. I was holding myself as if I were ready for battle, on guard duty for myself, my friends, my family, my clients. I let go, I took a deep breath. I am not that important. What a relief to not be held hostage by my history, my ego, and others expectations.

For part of this week, I was again at the mercy of my head. I was okay whenever I was fully engaged, usually when I was working, but some of the time, I was hanging out with some old voices that were giving me a hard time. I was feeling isolated and trapped in my roles. I believe that we play roles in life, and like good actors, we bring the authentic parts of ourselves that fit to each role. My roles of teacher, listener, facilitator, and writer are a privilege and give me incredible rewards; on the other hand, my personal roles of lover, boyfriend, and friend, sometimes get short shrift. Last week, I wanted to have someone to hold me, or make me dinner after an intense day.

We are all complicated and contradictory. I am content, busy, involved, smart, funny, sexy and humble (LOL); I am also complex, and, when my mind starts fucking with me, I feel at the mercy of my skewed perception of circumstances.

I have to practice everything I talk about with clients and in this book. I forget who I am. I forget that I am always okay when I am in the present. I forget that my life is filled with such grace and wonder. I forget… then, I remember.

The moment we notice that we have forgotten what we know, we are back. If we are curious, we stay present. If we judge, we are gone again. Curiosity is the antidote to judgment. The mind can't fuck with us when we are truly curious. Remember that!

Working on ourselves does not mean that we will not forget, but that we might remember faster! A client lamented that he had spent 48 hours obsessing over a guy he had been dating. My reply: "Only 48 hours! That's progress!"

We forget when we compare. We know that to compare ourselves to others is ridiculous, that we are comparing our insides to their outsides, but the most insidious comparison is usually with an idealized version of ourselves; that is, the "I" who is always graceful and knows exactly what to say and how to finesse any situation. Such an "I" doesn't exist.

This is the trap of perfectionism, an absolute guarantee for frustration: One must fail if you strive to be perfect. We need to lower the bar. My ex used to point out my desire to be perfect, and how it was not only hard on me, but on him, as he felt he was required to do the same. In response I came up with a new goal: Not to strive for perfection, to strive for excellence. Personal excellence is possible. We don't have to settle for mediocrity and we might even enjoy ourselves!

TRUTH OF ATTRACTION

Of late, I have been dating mostly younger men — much younger men.

People sometimes have "business" with each other; meaning they have a deep connection that they feel compelled to work out. That business can be about a moment or a month or a lifetime. One of the things that comes from "outliving myself" is the conviction that I will not turn away from that which brings me a feeling of aliveness. I can't worry about what other people will say.

When I was in my 20s, I had three significant relationships. One was brief but impactful with a 56-year-old man of the world. Although he had an Oscar and some Tonys, he did not seem to be enjoying his life fully, and I moved on, not ready to be engulfed in his not fully felicitous aura. Another was with a delightful Venezuelan director who was four years older than me; he was my inspiration to change continents at a whim and run off and be an artist. The most important was with the brilliant photographer, Peter Hujar, who was 16.5 years older than me, to the day: Our birthdays being exactly six months apart, October 11 and April 11.

Peter was a particularly insightful mentor. He taught me how to trust my "eye" and how to wash a dish. I was introduced to the best of outsider and avant-garde art: Charles Ludlam's Ridiculous Theatrical Company, Ethyl Eichelberger...some of the greats. Art was life and life was not always easy, but it was thrilling nonetheless.

My next major lover, a writer, was six years younger than me, and I taught him how to wash a dish and thrive in New York City. Over the ensuing decades, there have been some slightly older and some slightly younger. My last beloved ex, a high-energy director/artist/entrepreneur is ten years younger than me. I am more confident for knowing him; he is more able to partake of the joy of the present. In some sense, all my relationships were successful: I have always learned and grown.

My lovers have been my teachers, my comrades, my students. My attractions have shifted and changed over the years. Some lovers are white, some black. Right now I am enamored of a smart, sexy young Taiwanese architect. My taste is catholic and mutable, depending upon the person and the chapter in my life. Since my last relationship ended, I have come to see that not only am I often attracted to younger men, but a lot of them seem to want a 60-year-old man — as lover, friend, mentor, and various combinations thereof. It's convenient; it's mutually beneficial. They keep me in touch with enthusiasm and vitality; I hope I bring them the gift of my experience.

I am confident in my own viability as a man of this age, and I am thrilled when I am attracted to a man my age or older. Recently though, I have been dating younger men: 38, 24, 32, 27.... I was talking about this with a 25-year-old romantic friend a few months back, and he put it this way: Despite the differences in our ages and races and backgrounds, we make sense together. We are "soul mates." Societal expectations be damned, the truth of our connection is a fact to us.

"Act your age," I hear either directly or between the lines from some of my friends and associates. This is my age: I ride a Segway. I enjoy sex. I have friends from 22 to 90, and I am still willing to risk having my heart broken in order to feel it full. And I don't always act like this society's picture of an almost 60-year-old. I have better things to do with my time. Crucial to The New 60 is honoring what brings the feeling of aliveness.

WHY ARE WE WAITING?

Just 48 hours ago I was settling in with a good book, feet up, dog curled at my knee, when the phone rang:

"I need you, babe. Right now." (It was my ex, Christo.)

"Where are you?" I asked.

"I'm in Aunt Michele's apartment, and she's dead."

"Okay. I'm on my way."

For many years I lived around much illness and death from AIDS. Some of my close friends and I would joke about what music to play at our memorials, what keepsake we wanted from each other's collection. For a while I was the "designated die-er" in my circle. We often think we know who is going next. We don't.

Christo's Aunt Michele lived in the same building he does, a few floors below. He had found an unusual situation for her: The once twenty-two, now seven, cats paid for half the rent by their original people who left New York City after September 11. Some of the cats couldn't travel.

Michele had traveled. Born in Buffalo, New York, she later left an abusive husband in California and escaped with her five young children to Salt Lake City, where she created a career, bought a house, and got all the kids safely to adulthood. About fifteen years ago, when she was 50, she realized that they weren't moving out, so she left them, kept paying the mortgage, and moved to New York City.

She lived in the YWCA for two years until Christo found her the cat-sitting job. By then she had clients as a personal assistant and was living a wonderful life: opera, theater, travel. In the five years she was my aunt-in-law, she visited Italy, Turkey, and Berlin, not to mention spots around the United States. She hosted a Thanksgiving dinner for "strays," and she had adventures: One day she decided to go swimming in the Hudson River, not realizing this was unusual in New York City. There were police helicopters and a bit of drama. She was an innocent in the best sense: optimistic, curious, and always ready to reinvent herself.

The weekend before her sudden death she went to the beach with her teenage grandniece and grandnephew from Utah and took them to a midnight showing of The Rocky Horror Picture Show, and the night before she died she had dinner with the kids, Christo, his current boyfriend, and another dear friend. They laughed and ate and then walked home twenty-plus blocks along the Hudson River Park.

The next day she didn't show up for work. Christo found her that evening. He called me, and within an hour, eight of us had gathered. Before we called the police, in the best Judy Garland–Mickey Rooney "let's put on a show" style, we created a little ceremony to send Michele's spirit on her way: We had a Buddha that Christo and I brought back from Bali. Her grandnephew, being a Mormon, had a picture of Jesus. We had crystals and a magic wand and, thanks to Google, Catholic and Jewish prayers. As the resident (although lapsed) Jew, I read the kaddish, the prayer for the dead. As part of her reinvention, Michele had taken the Jewish name of her deceased stepfather. I always felt she wanted to be Jewish. A Mormon prayer rounded out our pantheistic service. We each chose a card from a "spirit card" deck and reminisced about Michele and read our cards: forgiveness, insight, farsightedness, discipline, wonder. We were amazed, as they summed up the gifts that Michele had given and continued to give to each of us.

Michele stunned us by leaving without a hint of warning. Bless her for reminding us that this life is fragile and not to be taken for granted. We do not yet know the cause of her death.

I do look for the lessons and gifts in everything that happens, however painful or challenging. My friends B. and T. are renting a flat in Paris for a month this fall. They have talked about it for years. Why now? Perhaps, because T.'s brother is dying of brain cancer. T. finally realized, "What am I waiting for?"

What are each of us "waiting for"? The art is to live as if this could be my last year and as if I will live to 90. Live fully now and plan for a possible future. Never count on anything ... anything is possible.

Michele was only five years older than I. AIDS didn't get me, but life will. I continue to strive to live as fully and gustily as Aunt Michele. And when it's my time, I'd like to pass on as gracefully.

REAL ESTATE IS
A LUXURY PROBLEM

Last week I was turned down by a New York City co-op board.

The reactions of my real estate agent, my lawyer, the mortgage loan officer at the bank, and my very best friends could be summed up by a shocked, "What the fuck?"

I was not shocked. I was surprised. However, what surprised me most was that I was merely disappointed rather than deeply upset.

I had placed every detail of my financial life (along with references and endorsements regarding my integrity, value to the community, and all-around charm) in the hands of a group of strangers so that they might judge. Me. On their terms.

I committed myself to getting this loft. My first offer was turned down. I was upset then. They chose another buyer "with better financials" who, ironically, couldn't get financing in the end, so they came back to me. I decided to go for it. There were obstacles:

Two mortgage brokers said I wouldn't qualify for a loan in this new marketplace. I kept at it anyway.

I am self-employed. My business expenses cancel out a significant portion of my income, and on paper, I don't fit into co-op board formulas.

Fitting in is not usually my number one goal. After a childhood and adolescence of trying to pass as "normal" (i.e., straight), by my 20s I had gone for a more noticeable style. I wore only white for many years and still tend to dress in light colors and wear a lot of cashmere scarves. I have often had long hair. I am one of only twelve who ride a Segway in Manhattan, which makes me an outlaw.

My work as a therapist came out of activism in the alternative healing community. We were the "lunatic fringe" in 1986: We were talking about living with HIV and quality of life. Today, I am doing the same work with HIV and other conditions, and it is considered "mainstream."

I have been employed in traditional jobs for a few months here and there, but the bulk of my work has been freelance: as a performer in New York, Italy, and Venezuela and on-screen; as the producer of theater and concerts and events; as a New York City taxi driver (I lasted six months); a waiter in Caracas; a sound engineer in Montreal. Life has been more an adventure than a fiscal road map. Retirement plans and mortgages and co-op boards were not high priorities.

Going for something is easy. Not getting attached to the outcome is not so easy.

One of the principles I use in my practice of living is a four-word affirmation given to me by a buddy, Steve Evans, before his death from AIDS in 1989: "totally committed/ completely unattached."

I always hope I can hold on to this principle.

I got into playing at real estate as I turned 40. The buying and selling and redesigning of properties is how I have made whatever capital I have accumulated. I have owned homes in Santa Fe and on Long Island. I have owned land in Brazil and the Dominican Republic, and two apartments in New York City. After September 2008, I knew I would have a challenge finding a mortgage even though all three of my credit ratings are in the 800s and I have successfully paid off three mortgages, never once late for a payment. Luckily, my bank came through for me. There are still banks that honor their relationships with their clients, I am happy to report.

This board didn't get me. As much as I might have seen this as a defeat, I am glad I went whole hog plus the postage for it. Commitment is my antidote to regret.

And I have no regrets. How can I? I have learned a lot from the experience. I understand my financial stats better. I realize the value of my credit rating. I am grateful for my assets.

I am writing this in Rio, on a trip I planned before I heard of the space. I am participating in the opening of my ex's company's Brazilian tour. My dog and I will spend the last days of August on the North Fork of Long Island. Big deal, I won't be moving this month to a loft on 27th Street.

I am almost 60. I almost died 16 years ago. Someone in my life died suddenly just ten days ago. Real estate is a luxury problem, not something to be attached to.

Playing outside the box means that some folks just don't get my game. Fitting in to please them would be too high a price to pay. Another loft awaits me ... a condo, I imagine. One with an outdoor space, okay? Striving to be totally committed/completely unattached, I begin anew.

HERE TO INSPIRE

The terrific It Gets Better video spots combating gay teen suicide make it clear: We are out of the Dark Ages, but the Age of Enlightenment has yet to come. Most of these videos make me cry (though I eventually smile through my tears). The Gay Men's Chorus of Los Angeles singing "True Colors" had me sobbing. There is unbearable beauty in connecting to the pain of our tribe, to the pain of all outsiders, the pain of humankind.

This is a pain I don't usually visit. My life as a gay adult has been easy. I almost forget that at 18, I too thought of suicide. I had almost passed as "normal" in school, but the effort was wearing me out. The first person to call me a fag was my mother. I knew that I had to toe the line in my family of overachieving Jewish jocks. Part of the problem was that I didn't even consciously realize I was gay. There were no gay role models. I had hoped that leaving home and going to college would fix my sense of disconnectedness. Initially, the atmosphere was even more conservative than at my high school. My first lifeline, my freshman year, was meeting other "freaks" at a weekend retreat for inner-city volunteers. I began to feel part of a community of outsiders. By the time I fully understood I was gay, a couple of years later, I was ready to see it as a creative opportunity: I'm not going to be living the life I was brought up to live, so I'm going to make the whole thing up. An early moment of truth and freedom.

I graduated and joined the world of theater and avant-garde arts. No one really cared about my sexuality. All were accepted, differences were celebrated, and I flourished. My family, in the long run, came through: My happiness was what they wanted. It was my job to find it, not theirs.

AIDS brought the true challenges. First there was terror: Will it be me? Then it was activism: I'll save myself by being at the front lines. Then it was me: Live for now. And then I outlived myself. I doubted, however, that I would ever have a partner again, that I would ever feel sexy again, that I would ever believe that a future was possible. And then it did get better: The life I am living today — gay, HIV-positive, and at the top of my game as I reach 60.

Some of my sadness at seeing these It Gets Better spots is that they are still needed.

Activism has been successful in part. I am proud to have presented the first production of the play that introduced the brilliant James Lecesne's *Trevor* to the world. Now the Trevor Project, the crisis intervention and suicide prevention organization for LGBTQ teens, is saving lives. What I am perhaps proudest of is that I may have provided a safer context for my gay nephew's childhood and coming of age. By living my life as an out gay man, I laid the groundwork so that he, the Lambda Literary Award–winning author of Boy Meets Boy, David Levithan, would never have to worry whether his family would accept him. He once told me that when he was 9 years old, he looked around the apartment I shared with my then-partner, Mark, and thought, two men, one bed; I get it.

Thankfully, we now have hundreds of out role models. A quantum leap from the Dark Ages, a.k.a. my childhood.

The New 60 is about it getting better as we age. Again, I was lucky; my father at 60 was vital and active. He and my uncles were role models for aging with vitality into their 70s, 80s, and 90s. Not everyone gets that.

So, young (and not so young) men and women, LGBTQ, straight, whatever: It does get better, as we get to know who we are and embrace pride, not bias against us. Whether we realize it or not, we are all role models: Speak up and take action. Come out if you can. Don't lie about your age. Be proud of your ethnicity, your sexuality, your gender, your body type, your unique qualities. The consistent theme of It Gets Better is that the very traits that make you an outsider when young bring you joy later in life! Survive. Thrive. Celebrate.

TAKING STOCK

Approaching a new decade includes taking stock of one's self and one's life. What's working and what isn't.

There is a wonderful exercise I learned from my brilliant colleague, Eric Schneider.

Project three years into the future and describe, in the present tense, your life as you want it to be. Really go for it, within the realm of possibility. If I say I am playing shortstop for the Yankees, it ain't gonna happen, but if I say I have a book on The New York Times best-seller list — possible. Include every aspect of your life: home, family, health, career, travel, relationship. Write it as if it already is.

When we envision ourselves clearly in this way, we have a touch-stone: Do my current actions match my goal? If not, do I really want it, or am I afraid of it?

If I am being honest with myself, the area that has me puzzled right now is relationships; particularly my desire for a long-term one. At lunch with my ex today, he challenged me to look at what I hadn't dared to admit I wanted while we were together. I had feared that if I revealed my needs and desires, it would be too clear he couldn't meet them. I believe I was afraid the truth would end our relationship. Now that we are no longer lovers, it seems foolish not to have taken that risk.

In preparation for my next relationship, it would be useful and daring to admit to myself what I want.

What stands between me and my future man? Well, first of all, there's my "picker" (I just heard this expression). I tend to pick men who are likely to not be fully committed by reason of character, age, or geography. My resistance to intimacy and surrender in a relationship has been masked by what seems to be, on the surface, the resistance and fears of the other — the perfect decoy for my resistance and fear.

My big secret: I actually want a romantic monogamous relationship. I want a man who can challenge me, see through my defenses, and know that I am worth the trouble it might take. He will also have to:

Be smart.
Make me laugh.
Get my sense of humor.
Be physically fit.
Be sexually adventurous.
Be an artist or have an artist's sensibility.
Have a spiritual awareness and/or practice.
Be passionate about life, work, service, art, family.

Have voted for Obama.

Have a career. Make a living.

Love my dog!

Be totally out and be comfortable with my visibility as a gay, HIV-positive man.

Be between 40 and 60, ideally.

Some of my list is negotiable; some is not: I can be with a man whether he is HIV-positive or not. I can't be with a man who voted for George W. Bush. I can be in an open relationship; I can't be with a heavy smoker. He can be wild; he cannot do crystal meth.

What are your nonnegotiables?

Projecting three years in the future, September 2013:

I am in my loft overlooking the river. Sophie, my Labrador, is lying on the terrace as the sun sets. I am making dinner, pasta and salad, for my partner, who is returning home from a business trip abroad. I am excited to see him and glad to have this evening in our home to catch up, connect, make love, and plan a trip to Asia for next spring.

My book, *The New 60*, is selling well in paperback, and I am writing for *O, the Oprah Magazine* again, as well as other magazine columns. I have a syndicated television show.

Next week I am hosting a family gathering: brothers, sisters-in-law, nieces and nephews and spouses and children and favorite cousins. It's time for us all to hang out and share our luck and love.

SAYING YES TO THE TRUTH

Saying yes to the truth is not always easy. I was brought up in a world of secrets. We were, on the surface, a perfectly regular family. But, looking back, we had an odd relationship with truth and reality. Unpleasant events were omitted from the record. My grandfather died of cancer, so we were told. Not true. My uncle had a different last name than his brothers. Why? He changed it to get jobs that Jews couldn't get. Not true. The list goes on and on,

Carrying secrets and lies can be tiring. Mark Twain said, "The great thing about telling the truth is that you don't have to remember what you said." Amen.

Traditionally, psychotherapists hold the confidences and secrets of their clients. I have been well trained in this art. Yet as a writer I am out to reveal my truth. Is this a conflict? Not really: My clients' business is sacrosanct; my own can be shared. Is a psychotherapist supposed to be a blank slate on which the client projects their view of the world, or an embodied human being? I am seeking to find a balance here, and I'm still working it out.

Recently I was asked to hold a secret I couldn't contain. It paralleled a family secret that I have hated carrying for almost thirty years. At this point, revealing it would, I believe, cause more harm than good. However, to be asked to begin to hold such a secret again felt unbearable. I followed the path of truth and was loyal to myself and my nearest and dearest. This was very hard to do. I was being disloyal to my upbringing. I was, however, being true to what I believe is honest.

In this book I am trying to speak my truth. Revealing doubts and/or conflict goes against my training. Always show the best side of yourself, I was taught. However, this often leads to falsity. We all have issues, and most of us have traumas to work out. Our process, our imperfection, is a significant part of our gift to the world. Occasionally we need to stand naked emotionally and allow for the complications and messiness of life.

Turning 60 is obviously big for me. I want to reach young men to let them know that getting older is more a plus than a loss. I miss my young skin, but the rest of aging is about things getting better. I have tools. I can choose the challenge of telling the truth as fast as I can — to myself and others. I can be disloyal to my lineage and true to myself.

Showing writing to friends opens one to instant feedback. I know that not everyone will appreciate my point of view. I am interested in those who disagree. And it is fascinating that some readers have trouble with my statements about liking myself and my life. I consider my contentment a hard-earned prize, the payoff for years of study and reflection. This is why getting older is so cool: If we continue to learn and grow, living does get better. Some people are born with the grace of inner peace. Most of us have to peel away the layers of indoctrination and embrace the peace that is our birthright.

There is always work to do. I like learning. I like being challenged. I struggle when my history gets in the way of my present by skewing perception. The alternatives to embracing the aging process are really daunting: resignation, despair, enervation.

The heart and mind and psyche are like the body — they thrive on exercise and healthy fuel. The regimen must be reevaluated periodically and adjusted for stress factors and changes in the circumstances of one's life. To maintain health, we continue to eat, drink, and move. Writing about approaching 60 allows me to examine the journey thus far, evaluate my practices and beliefs, and adjust for drift.

I am so fortunate: I love this life that I have worked for ... yes!

LIVING WELL

My niece asked me if I had seen *The Bucket List* when it was out a few years ago. "I've been living it, my dear" was my instant reply. I have lived at an accelerated pace for most of the last fifteen years. It has been great. I have traveled, created a career or two, and had wonderful lovers. No regrets. And the next learning edge is usually enhanced by doing things differently: To put it simply, it's time to do less and be more.

This came up for me at a retreat for gay caregivers this past weekend. It was refreshing to be among men, gay men, who have gone beyond many of our society's prejudices and included sexual healing as part of their mission as therapists or body workers. I loved joining this particular subgroup of my tribe. I had gone there to explore adding new dimensions to my work as a therapist. Much to my surprise, I realized that I didn't need to expand my modalities. I needed to go deeper within the work I am already doing, personally and professionally.

One of my closest friends is in a six-week silent retreat. No books, no music, no writing. Dare I confront myself without distractions? The very idea of it is both thrilling and terrifying, an inner challenge, an inner journey. Now that's sitting on the edge of the unknown — mindfulness is at the core of everything that matters to me.

I have avoided that quiet space: Every time my life becomes peaceful, I have created a project, whether it's changing professions or buying an apartment or land in Brazil or the Dominican Republic. Being able to discern the difference between quiet contentment and boredom is a fine art that I have, up to now, lightly explored. It is time to commit. This will mean not letting opportunity take advantage of me. It might mean less travel, not changing domiciles for a while, having a less frantic romantic life, less drama.

I seem to have begun the process. I turned down the opportunity to buy an apartment this week. No hurry; I will move when it is time. My glass is overflowing with my work at Friends in Deed, my private practice, writing, and my relationships of various stripes.

I love to say yes! And at this point in time I have got to be able to say no.

"IT GETS BETTER"

I have outlived myself. Fifteen years ago today my T-cell count was 22. The other day my doctor told me my last count was 822. What a difference 800 makes. It's like money in the bank. Even better!

October 11, 1995, is the day I began an antiretroviral cocktail that I got by winning a lottery under a "compassionate access" program. Compassionate access translates in the pharmaceutical world as "you are so close to death that we don't follow all the rules."

The lottery existed because my friend Brenda, a passionate AIDS activist, had sat down a month earlier with the president of Merck, the maker of Crixivan, and when told that it worked, but we'd have to wait, she replied, "My son Brett died five years ago. My son Michael is dying now. I cannot wait." A lottery was created, and I was a winner (of the 100 people in my doctor's office who entered, three of us won). Now I know that I would have gotten the meds within a few months, but then it was like winning $10 million.

I am still here to write about it. I am halfway, exactly, between my 59th and my 60th birthdays. What do I need to say that is still unsaid? Readers are helping. Recently I was chided for what I was leaving out of my writing. A lot of what I leave out is about sex and sexuality and sexual healing. As a therapist, as a gay man, as an American, I have internalized a lot of prejudices about sexual expression. I like to think of myself as the "guilt-free" therapist: able to hold most anything my clients put before me with compassion, curiosity, and without judgment. Again and again, the most liberal and socially conscious people still judge the sexual behavior of others and/or themselves. This is sad. If my silence is complicity, it is even sadder.

I have worked to free myself of a good deal of inhibition. I enjoy my body. I enjoy sex. I enjoy sex with other men.

I have been advised by well-meaning friends who read my writing to tone down the sex: "A little sex goes a long way." Perhaps, and maybe that is just a subtle way of holding back, of not acknowledging who I am and what I really do.

It's pretty simple: I have more sex than most of my friends and acquaintances (and the quality of it seems to be higher as well, in many cases). I expect to be attacked for this statement as I have before when I put it in print. I've heard, "you are tall and thin and blah blah blah ...."

Well, last week I sat and spoke with a man I knew thirty years ago, He is writing about Peter Hujar, the cult photographer who was my lover in the '70s. The writer and I are the same age: He is heavyset, round, balding, not tall, and he said the most wonderful thing, "Not since my 20s, when I was cute, have I felt as attractive as I feel now. I am sought after in the most surprising way by many men who want me just as I am."

I am convinced that at least 80% of our sexual attractiveness comes from how we feel about ourselves. Come on, we all know men who are not classically attractive who are irresistible to men and/or women. We also know physical beauties who lack sexiness and are basically celibate.

A few of us are born or bred with sexual confidence; most of us have to claim it. I put myself in the latter category. Assisting people in finding their inner beauty and comfort in their skin is a mission.

The saddest comment on my writing came from the eminent gay/ AIDS activist Larry Kramer, who said, "Most gay men, I more and more believe, don't have much sex at all, or any, certainly not enough, but live lives, as Thoreau said, 'of quiet desperation.' ... I think it is impossible for any gay man to have sex today without the sword of Damocles hanging over their head."

I disagree with Larry on this. Of course it's true for some. It is not true for many, and I want it not to be true for more. I know that it is possible to be gay, HIV-positive, and 60 and have a wonderful fulfilling sexual life.

When in my practice and at Friends in Deed I meet terrified newly diagnosed HIV-positive men who think they can't have a full life or follow their dreams, I can honestly tell them that although I cannot promise anything specific, I know it is possible. I have been HIV-positive for almost thirty years and I am living a wonderful, challenging, full life, including the realization of many of my dreams.

Those of us who are elders have a responsibility. Prejudice and internalized prejudice kills. I just left a vigil in Washington Square to mark the tragic recent loss of four gay teens to bullying-prompted suicides. We must speak up and say, "Yes, it does get better ... hold on, there are wonderful possibilities for your future." There's the new 20, the new 30, the new 60 ... ahead!

THE NORMAL HEART

The other night I saw a brilliant 25th anniversary reading of Larry Kramer's The Normal Heart. This play is not only a powerful historical tragedy, but timely. It directly and indirectly addresses the costs of prejudice and internalized prejudice, looking at hatred and self-hatred and the cost therein of countless lives.

Society's prejudices are everywhere. We absorb them, and subtly or not so subtly we build up belief systems about ourselves based on what we are exposed to and experience. Sadly, we often buy into the idea that we are "less than" because of something we are. Prejudice can be truly insidious, and the good news is that we have a great deal of influence on its healing, since it's about a change in our own perceptions, not about changing others.

I doubt that any of us are without some level of internalized homophobia, racism, classism, AIDS-phobia, sexism, or whatever applies individually.

The first time I led a workshop on internalized prejudice, as preparation, a colleague and I asked ourselves, "Where am I operating out of internalized prejudice?" After a pause, she laughed and said, "Even though my mother knows I'm gay and loves my long-term partner, whenever I go to visit I pack my most feminine clothes ... and always wonder why I feel like I have nothing to wear!" Then it was my turn. To my surprise, what came up was not about my sexuality or HIV status. "When people say to me that they don't think I'm Jewish, I have always taken it as a compliment." This is my internalized anti-Semitism. I know where it comes from. My grandmother's family prided themselves on their ability to "pass" as gentile and to secure jobs that Jews couldn't get in early-20th-century America.

In the face of virulent prejudice and bigotry there is often real danger: gay bashings, prosecution, job loss, etc. I am not suggesting that people put themselves in harm's way. However, we are often reacting emotionally as if we are in danger when actually we are in a very safe environment.

In workshops, participants often ask how we can let go of internalized prejudice. The first step is always discovery, followed by observation. For example, within months of discovering my internalized anti-Semitism, more than one friend said to me, "You are acting 'more Jewish' than you used to." When asked what they meant by this, they said I was using more Yiddish, talking about my European maternal grandparents, and even speaking in dialect when telling a joke. I was thrilled and fascinated. The act of discovery had begun a change in my perspective as evidenced in my behavior. It can be that simple.

And the list of internalized prejudices is as broad as prejudice itself.

Internalized homophobia can lead to isolation, being in the closet, even suicide. We are all role models for having survived childhood and the often difficult teen years. It is important to be outspoken about the good things that come from being older, gay, Jewish, Muslim, a person of color, or any of the characteristics that leads to people separating themselves from one another. Most of our young people are not hearing enough positive statements about what they are now, or eventually will be.

AIDS-phobia causes too many people to not be tested for HIV. At Friends in Deed, I still work with men and women who had developed AIDS before testing. Their beliefs about HIV stigma endanger their health and well-being. Ignorance is bred by fear and reinforced by internalized shame.

Most of us have significant degrees of internalized ageism. Except for 20-year-olds, most of us are delighted to hear that we look ten years younger than our numerical age.

We can fight ageism by telling the truth about our age and gently reminding everyone, including ourselves, that this is what 40, 50, 60, 80 looks like. My dear friend Joe is 90, and within the past year he has traveled to Europe and Asia, on his own. He is one of my inspirations for aging with style.

Back in 1985, The Normal Heart was prescient about ways that our self-esteem is undermined, making a case for gay marriage, addressing teen suicide, and even referring to gays in the military. We have an obligation to continue to speak out and act whenever the seeds of internalized prejudice are being planted or fertilized. It's a matter of life and death. However, let's not only survive, let's thrive as who and what we are. This is our gift to the world.

STRONG AND VULNERABLE

When I was in my 20s I had a much older lover, the photographer Peter Hujar, who was about 15 years younger than I am today. He changed my life the day I met him by saying, "I am looking for someone who is strong enough to be vulnerable." Peter died on Thanksgiving Day, 1987. He was 53. Strong and vulnerable.

So often, in workshops and therapy sessions, clients express fear that they are being weak by being vulnerable. Peter opened the door to an opposite view. Our authentic selves, our power and being, are expressed in all our emotions. What strength it takes to be open and honest and, yes, vulnerable. Fake strength is mired in machismo and a facade of toughness, which is overcompensation for fear. We all experience fear. Big deal.

Our experience of life is always about perception. We are so afraid that someone will not approve or, worse yet, mock our differences. Recently, two friends talked about their issues of masculinity as it relates to their dogs. One friend, a hypermasculine man of 50, admitted that walking his white Pekingese was embarrassing. He felt like he was waving an "I'm gay" banner. Another friend, a striking figure, tattoos, shaved head with a tuft on the back, said that he wouldn't carry his Jack Russell Terrier because it would feel too gay.

Internalized machismo once again. These men were talking about walks in the West Village and Soho. And yet I do remember walking that Pekingese and wanting to hold up a sign that said, "My dog is a yellow Lab." The persecution of gays is usually tied to the prejudice against perceived "sissies."

A wonderful post on Facebook by a mother proudly defending her 5-year-old son's choice to be a female cartoon character on Halloween caused so many to yell "Bravo!" And to opine that we need more mothers and fathers like her.

When I was 9, I dressed as a girl for Halloween. My father wouldn't let me out the door. My mother agreed: "He enjoys it too much." I never did drag again. I was careful as a boy, then as a young man, to "pass." In our culture there are rewards for "passing" as white or gentile or younger or straight. What if I slipped and did something feminine? Then it was terrifying. Now it wouldn't matter: I might receive some odd looks from strangers and prejudiced friends, but I might even be appreciated for it. Maybe next Halloween, I'll be Krystle Carrington from Dynasty; my big shoulders would be hidden under those '80s shoulder pads!

Compensation by doing drag is not required. I do, however, salute the drag queens and the unrepentant sissies out there. They are often discriminated against by their gay brothers. It saddens me to see men advertising online that they are "straight-acting." Let's not "act." Once again, let's be who we are: flamboyant, conservative, bourgeois, radical, masculine, feminine, fluid, etc…

I used to like it when people assumed that I was a trust-fund baby by virtue of my privileged lifestyle, education, and speech (thank you, Aunt Gladys, for the elocution lessons when I was a child). One day a friend who was really born "with a silver spoon in her mouth" startled me into another life-shifting truth. I had been saying that my father had quit school at 14 to support his family and was a New York City cop during the Depression before going into the restaurant business, that all four of my grandparents were born in Europe, and that my family came here in the late 19th and early 20th centuries, penniless, fleeing persecution. She said, "Who you are is so much more interesting than what I had thought."

The most interesting thing we have to offer is the truth of our journey.

Our culture will attempt to seduce us to abandon ourselves and pretend to be who someone says we should be. The New 60 is my opportunity to leave behind inhibitions and made-up fears, and flaunt my unique qualities — shouting, whispering, giggling — if not now, when?

MELANCHOLIC HOLIDAYS

Fucking Holidays! I have never been a bah-humbugger, but this year I realized that something had changed. I was surprisingly melancholic: Why? I was childless (not new), parentless (not new), and partnerless (new). I have begun to notice that when childless, single clients of a certain age lose their last parent, there is often a seismic shift in their world. Not everyone feels these things. I hadn't expected to be one who does. Wrong again. I feel somewhat unmoored. Siblings and nieces and nephews and friends fill the void, but there is still that biological/karmic hole, no blood relation immediately above or below.

My father, the amazing Lou, died just before Thanksgiving five years ago. My brothers and my extended family have been ever-present, before and after. However, this was my first Thanksgiving without my ex. In the past, we had trekked to Jersey, the Upper West Side, Salt Lake City. This year he was working and I was with a delightful gathering of friends in Brooklyn. I missed him ... I missed us.

My mood wasn't helped by Thanksgiving being the anniversary of the death of a beloved once-upon-a-time lover, or that my ex's aunt who died mysteriously this past summer always hosted Thanksgiving (we went to her before going to my family). Loss. Getting older does include continuing losses.

In the last year, a new grandniece was born, two of my nieces have been engaged, and there is a grandnephew in utero. Gains!

I have written about being newly single. I do expect to have another partner and all that that will bring. Being childless is a bigger issue I realize, as it is not something that is likely to change.

I remember when I came out to my mother. The first words out of her mouth: "You would've been such a wonderful father!" My response: "I don't preclude having children."

"Oh, you might adopt," she said.

"Or have my own," was my immediately rejoinder, to her immense surprise.

Having a child was not something I was going to give up just because I was gay. I was in my 20s, so I didn't have to figure it out right away. Today, it would be a no-brainer; adoption, surrogacy, egg donor, whatever. We weren't so sophisticated in the '70s. By the time I was ready to seriously consider fatherhood, AIDS had entered the picture. I mourned losing the chance to be a biological father because of my HIV-positive status (again, today, it would be doable). I also hesitated to imagine adopting, as my own lifespan was so particularly unpredictable. Now both my brothers are grandfathers, and I'm not that much younger than they. I'd like to just skip to being a grandfather!

Being childless is not a gay issue. It is also not necessarily a default position. I know happily married heterosexual couples in their 70s and 40s and 30s who have chosen not to have children. Let us not forget that there are too many people on this planet.

Besides, when the wishful parent talks about having a child, they are usually imagining healthy, well-adjusted children who bring joy and satisfaction. We don't usually sign on for the hard realities that often come with parenthood. Some of my friends joke ruefully about it — "What was I thinking?" — as they struggle with the emotional and financial drain of troubled adult children. In most cases, aging parents are no picnic either.

I invest a lot of energy in my friendships and my family. It's time to put even more energy into the multigenerational aspect of my life. Next year I just might say yes to my brother's Thanksgiving invitation to Hilton Head, South Carolina, with his sons, daughter-in-law, and three grandchildren. When I traveled to Europe with his sons and eldest granddaughter a decade ago, the trip was, as hoped for, bonding. I will always remember my grandniece, Paige, at 18 months old, on my hip as I made espresso in the kitchen of that Tuscan villa. I have that memory. She at least knows the photographs.

My other brother is particularly adept at staying in touch as well. And I have truly extraordinary friends! In a sense I am well taken care of. I just lack those grandkids.

In the midst of writing this, I went to have dinner with one of my cool nieces. We were discussing being parentless (which she is not) and childless (which she currently is). We talked about the possibility of her having a child on her own if Mr. Right doesn't come along in the next few years. As she discussed her concern about her support system for single motherhood, I found myself given the opportunity to really look at being a "grandparent" to her not-yet-conceived child, a full-out commitment of time and resources. I offered this as an option. I fully expect that she will meet the father of her children, but you never know.

As often happens, when I let myself explore my sadness or feelings of lack, I find myself buoyed by all that I do have, all the possibilities. A wise friend taught me that the glass is neither half full nor half empty, it is both. Life is full and empty; light and shadow; love and suffering. I am singular and part of a family. I live alone and I have community.

Living and loving fully allow us to be delighted and dismayed all at once.

PERFECTLY FLAWED

Most Sundays, I can be found at table sixty at Hundred Acres Restaurant in SoHo. I have lived on an upper floor of its building for a while. I meant to stay a year or so between selling and buying spaces. To my surprise, this past summer, when a real estate deal collapsed, I was actually relieved. I love living here. The restaurant is a second home. My father had restaurants. Being on a first-name basis with the staff, having a regular table, and known likes (club soda with lemon arrives without placing an order) feels like my childhood revived.

I also enjoy mixing my friends. I would entertain at home more when I lived in a bigger space. I had cocktails for forty or dinner for sixteen. Now I use the restaurant as my "dining club."

Today we were six: a long-married couple, a gay couple who have been together in some form since they were teenagers in Kentucky, a divorced Turkish designer, and me. As is often the case, some were acquainted, some had not met, and yet I trusted that the conversation would be lively, touching on life, the world situation, style, and silliness. We are as likely to discuss a play, a sweater, the business climate in China, or yachting on the Turkish coast as the merits of the excellent brunch. Next week it'll be a different crew, some repeats, maybe a wild card or two.

Tomorrow night I am having dinner with my friend Joe, who turned 91 yesterday. On Friday, I spent time with a 24-year-old. Last night I had a date with a 43-year-old actor. Tonight I am seeing the final performance of *The Scottsboro Boys* on Broadway with my ex and his lover. To quote, once again, my friend Felicity: "I only add, I never subtract!" Friendship and romance and family can blend and intermix: all ages and backgrounds, the newly met and the lifelong-cherished. In part, this is how I deal with being childless and single.

I also work within a community. Last Tuesday night I sat in a big group at Friends in Deed and marveled at the level of discourse among the close to forty men and women who had chosen to be there on a chilly December evening. Even though most of them were dealing with crisis in their lives, there was a sense of well-being, a sense of belonging, a sense of the shared journey. It is a privilege to be in the presence of such honesty and courage. It amazes me that I am invited into the internal journey of some of these clients. Being a therapist is like going into a novel's structure, the plot line, and working to facilitate new patterns, passages, and potential outcomes. Working within the mystery, we attempt transformation, often successfully. Wow!

I write a lot about luck and fortune. Fortune, as a wise friend explained to me a couple of years ago, is different from luck. Fortune is when we take luck and apply it; put it to good use. I have been lucky, and I am fortunate. Having a full social and professional network requires both good fortune and effort. I invest in relationships because they sustain me, personally, professionally, and spiritually. Our lives reflect our choices. In order to compensate for the lack of my own children, and at present, a partner, I need to reach out, mingle, and create social opportunities that reflect my comfort levels and ambitions. I would rather give a party than attend one, so I like to host. I enjoy live performance, so I buy pairs of tickets and invite a friend. I accept invitations from friends and colleagues that reinforce our connection. Therefore, when I am overwhelmed or disappointed, I have people to turn to and they have me.

I am fortunate to have created a life that is multidimensional, rich, and perfectly flawed. Recently I was feeling at the mercy of the holidays. Today I am willing to celebrate life and the spark of love that illuminates it amidst the dark moments.

To luck, to love, to good fortune and joy. Happy New Year.

BE HERE NOW

The other afternoon I was checking e-mail at an Internet café in Grenada, the Caribbean island the United States invaded in the Reagan years. A friend request from Facebook led me to log on to that site. Oh, what the hell, I thought, I'll post my whereabouts and "next stop Bequia," a small and rather unknown isle in the Grenadines.

The next morning I rose early for snorkeling and noticed that I had a text message from my friends Rob and Debs, "We're in Bequia." I had met this energetic and thoroughly charming couple a few years ago at Christmas on the remote island of Boipeba in Brazil. The following year we were all in South Africa together, and last year it was Búzios, again in Brazil. We are currently planning a boat charter in Turkey this coming June. All this to explain that we usually know each others' whereabouts at the holidays, but we'd had a gap in communication. So, thanks to Facebook and texting, I spent a lovely afternoon with them at their rented villa in the hills above Bequia's exquisite harbor. Sometimes modern technology is amazing,

I used to describe myself as a Luddite (the term comes from a radical British anarchist group that tried to impede the Industrial Revolution by throwing sandals into the machinery and stopping the factories from functioning. Obviously, they didn't succeed at halting industrialization). I had held out against being online until a clever group of friends gave me an iBook for my 50th birthday, and soon I came to love not only writing on my computer, but e-mail and online access to other gay men. I actually met my last partner on a dating site! Yet when we met, six years ago, I was adamant, "I can run my business and life with a fountain pen." My resistance broke down step by step. Now I have a website; use Google and YouTube daily; am Linked In; and have thousands of "friends" on Facebook!

Language acquisition is an apt metaphor for my relationship with technology. Those born after 1980 or so grew up speaking computer and cell phone, etc. I, who went to college with an electric typewriter, am learning the language of technology as an adult. I can hope to be conversant if I work at it, but I will never be mistaken for a native speaker. Learning Spanish in my youth and Italian in college were much easier than when I studied Portuguese in my 50s. It's a challenge to be a beginner at my age. A worthwhile challenge, I am finally ready to wholeheartedly admit and embrace.

Technology is neutral. How we use it is not. I am disturbed by seeing so many people, particularly the young, absorbed by their devices as they walk the streets or even, as I saw yesterday, sailing on a catamaran in the Caribbean. They're missing the experience of being where they are. As a society, we are losing touch with our context.

Right now my context is writing on my iPad in my cabin on a ship. I have some anxiety, as this is a new device for me and I am not yet able to ensure that this piece will not be lost by an errant click. Pad and paper have a certain reliability. MobileMe will eventually put this into cyber storage. That boggles my mind. If I had showed up with this device or my iPhone thirty years ago it would have been like having a Wizard's wand. When I am impatient, as I was at the cybercafé yesterday, with the slowness of the PC, I try to remind myself that I am being impatient with a miracle.

I have friends who resist technology and decry its danger to our well-being. I absolutely sympathize with such concerns. However, like the Industrial Revolution, the information age is here until the next yet-unknowable breakthrough. Of course we need to hone our awareness of the pull toward losing touch with the present and our context. It is our duty to mitigate its dangers and to use its abilities to create connection, peace, understanding, and good. Age doesn't have to be a dividing line. I know 90-year-olds who use e-mail and cell phones. I know much younger folks who in their resistance are becoming caricatures of ungraceful aging. I am grateful for the fluency of the young as I stumble, at times, in this new language. As I strive to expand my technological acumen I also strive to uphold the poetry of my native tongue, remembering to switch my devices off and simply "be here now."

Photo by Peter Hujar

THE QUALITY OF LIFE IS NOT DETERMINED BY THE CIRCUMSTANCES

There is a well-known photograph of me by Peter Hujar, taken when I was 26. In it I am bending over, seemingly on my way to touching the floor with my hands. Actually, at 26, I couldn't touch the floor. I can now!

These days I am flipping, hanging upside down, doing my own version of moves created for Pink and Mariah Carey. My shoulder is no longer frozen, and I can bend in most directions. My first serious yoga practice was when I was nearing 40. During that period I was able to put my flat palms on the floor. In the last couple of years, AntiGravity Yoga has brought me even more flexibility. I am amazed! I had taken my progress for granted until my AntiGravity Yoga teacher began to vociferously point it out, saying, "You rock."

When I was 21, I was told that it was too late for me to start dancing seriously. I ended up in Twyla Tharp's company five years later. In 1994, I was told I would be dead in five years. I'm still here

Authority figures ("They say") often tell us what we can and cannot do. Please stop listening and find out for yourself. Our limitations are, of course, real, but they are also individual, often changeable — if we are willing to put in the necessary sweat and practice.

Beliefs are like statistics. They're about groups, not individuals. One of the characteristics of resilience, both physical and psychological resilience, is unreasonableness. Being unreasonable means going against standard wisdom. I was diagnosed with AIDS when the received wisdom of the era was, "You will be dead in two to three years." My family simply said, "If anyone can beat this, you can — be unreasonable." My family was pretty nutsy in some respects, however, when it came to resilience, they were brilliant teachers. My Aunt Estelle was told in her very early 30s that she was too infirm to be a New York City schoolteacher, a job she loved. Later that year she was critically ill and nearly died. As part of her recovery, she went to law school, then practiced for 50 years and died approaching 90, after becoming a case study for her doctors.

So now, when someone says that a man my age should or shouldn't (fill in the blank), I question it and, if interested, explore it for myself. There are physical challenges that I have yet to meet: parachute, scuba dive. I'd like to ski again. On January 1, I zip-lined through the rain forest on St. Lucia. What's the problem? I am only turning 60.

I feel at the top of my game physically, professionally, and sexually. No one ever told me this was what 60 would look like. And I know that it isn't true for everyone. My body hurts at times. Advil and massage and rest are required. Just when I think I may not be able to expand my limits much more, I can have a new discovery. To maintain my physique, I must go to the gym regularly, lifting weights and doing some cardio. My dog has me walking many miles a week. I eat reasonably well and take vitamins and supplements. I am focused on maintenance with windows of growth, and I am loving it.

More and more we are looking at a new paradigm for aging. There are factors that inhibit talking about it, however. God forbid that one seems to be bragging about fitness or well-being. What if it makes someone who is in poorer shape feel bad? These attitudes come from scarcity and are limiting. The full range of experience, extraordinary or challenging, validates the exceptional and helps to expand our point of view.

Pushing our boundaries as we age can also be inhibited by societal values, internalized ageism, and often the discomfort of being a beginner. In order to learn to fly with AntiGravity Yoga, I had to be a humble newbie. If our egos get organized around our "advanced" status, we are held back. It is often necessary to be uncomfortable and awkward on the way to soaring breakthroughs.

My dictum for years has been, "The quality of life is not determined by the circumstances." If I am to live by this, then I have to work to thrive within my circumstances as I strive to help others make the most of theirs.

Let's be in the present with our state of being, exercising our physical and psychic muscles with curiosity and joy.

RADICAL ROLE MODELS

The moment I realized I was gay, I also realized that I was going to get to make my life up. If I wasn't going to lead the life I was raised to live, let my new life be a creative opportunity.

I also grew up in an era when the best things about being gay were that you didn't have to serve in the army (provided you were courageous enough to be out) and you didn't have to get married. I find I am gaining my rights, but am I losing my privileges in the process?

The phenomenon of the first baby boomers turning 65, my oldest brother among them, has me examining my generational heritage. As an activist, I am thrilled by the coming end of "don't ask, don't tell," and I cheer whenever a state grants marriage rights. However, as a hippie generation Vietnam War protester, I am perplexed by how traditional this all seems.

Actually, I'd like to see the end of marriage: Civil unions for all who want them, and marriage as a religious or social rite. As to the military, I know it sounds pie-in-the-sky and more than a bit naive, but I'd like to place metaphoric daisies in all the rifles and refocus on slogans such as, "War Is Unhealthy for Children and Other Living Things!"

Our economy is top-heavy with military expenditures and under-weighted toward art, nature, education, and their intersection. If Brazil and so many European nations, for example, can see arts funding as vital, then so can we. When I sold a house years ago and had $30,000 in capital gains tax, I despaired that I was possibly paying for one tire on a fighter plane. If I could have fed children or underwritten chamber music for toddlers, I'd have written that check with joy. I am one of those people who wouldn't mind pay-ing taxes if I could earmark my giving. Therefore I use every loop-hole available and give money to works that make my heart sing: Friends in Deed, the Trevor Project, Doctors Without Borders, the Nature Conservatory, the American Civil Liberties Union, and Lambda Legal, to name a few.

Fuck the military budget. Fuck wars that solve nothing. And, please, enough with religion. I list myself on Facebook as a "free-range Buddhist" because I fear dogma and structure and "us" and "them." My great-uncle Joe, who was born in the 19th century, used to rant about burning down the churches and synagogues because they fomented hatred. Today, he would have added mosques to his list.

Call me unrealistic, call me an anarchist, call me bohemian, call me anything but a fundamentalist.

I am willing to give up the barefoot wedding in wrinkled linen on a beautiful sandy beach for the simple freedom to love and live and not kill. So let's take a break from tradition and look at creating something new. The American dream is prime for reinvention: two cars and 2.2 children is outdated. John Lennon's dream: Imagine all the people living life in peace.

I am impatient for post-gay culture. I have been looking to a younger generation to forge new visions of relationship and cooperation and peace that transcend gender and sexuality and race. We need to be pro-choice, pro-love, pro-peace, anti-homophobia, inclusive, and progressive.

And perhaps those of my generation who have survived have the opportunity and the obligation to recover our place as radical role models and do our part.

RISK JUNKIE

I'm a petty, ungrateful, sniveling whiner, reduced to self-pity by the flu. The co-diagnosis is entitlement. My perception has become so skewed that I perceive my high-octane life as a right — rather than a privilege. Whether I write this in dead seriousness or mere ironic dudgeon, how absurd my plaint!

Memory (probably inaccurate) tells me that I handled life-threatening illness with more grace. Why the big deal over the flu? I had to cancel workshops; I have missed Broadway performances and publication parties. I have had to ask for help from friends and neighbors and colleagues. So?

There is a wise spiritual teacher who frames life's challenges as "inconvenient." I have been down-sized: inconvenient; if my child is in jail without bail, that's very inconvenient; if I have inoperable cancer, that's very, very inconvenient. On this scale, the flu is a bad-hair day.

My mind doesn't follow this logic all of the time, however. While ill I was haunted by visions of a sudden decline into older age. Alone, living in a 4th floor walk-up, unable to care for my dog, and feeling marginalized. The New 60 is based on taking those stairs two at a time and having what a friend described the other night as "the best social network of anyone I know." But suddenly 4,000 Facebook friends don't seem as important as a spouse or an elevator.

Life is all perception. Today as my health has rebounded and I am feeling much better, I would like to skip over my less attractive musings of the past week, but they offer yet another fucking opportunity for growth. I am not as at ease with turning 60 as I would like to believe.

When I started writing this book eleven months ago, I think I assumed that by now I would have a new boyfriend, a new loft, and a slightly used convertible. I have had a lot of fun this year, so far — traveling and falling in and out of love and lust. I have been expanding the scope of my professional life through writing, and other endeavors. And, I have so much more work to do on myself.

When I was in graduate school, we were discussing emotional decoys, ways that clients hide their true feelings. My professor gave me a bit of gold, "You, Levithan," he said, "have a very interesting decoy; you reveal so much that what remains hidden is difficult to see." Bingo!

I have few qualms about revealing my story in all of its messy glory. Underneath, however, I am very, very private. The vault has been closed, to me as well as others. Turning 60 has begun to spring the lock. After all, what am I waiting for?

I have to admit that my life is mostly wonderful, and I also can admit that I have moments when I feel such isolation, that I dull this pain with work and thrills. Recently, one of my doctor's was asking me a series of lifestyle-related questions and I was struck by how they revealed an underlying addiction — risk. I am a risk junkie. I ride a Segway without a helmet, I love extreme sports, and I love to take risks with my heart. I embrace extreme physical pleasure. By working with people in crisis, I keep the day-to-day stakes high. What I fear is boredom.

The challenge of course is to differentiate between quiet contentment and boredom. One is peace, the other is hell, and my inability to discern the difference has become a handicap.

Our culture encourages distraction. It is not easy to get quiet and meet the demons, to observe the mind, and to realize that we are not the chatter. Illness forced me to listen, to hear the craziness, and to offer yet another chance to remember that I am not my thoughts or my feelings — that I am actually fine, with the flu, within the existential dilemma of being human.

When I was facing death from AIDS, I was often at my best. I need to go back to loving my mortality; to balancing my desire to live healthily until 90 with the very real possibility that this might be my last year on Planet Earth.

God grant me the serenity to accept the things I cannot change, the courage to change the things I can, and the wisdom to know the difference.

MEN COME WITH WARNING LABELS

"Men come with warning labels," my friend Sally Fisher wisely quipped. "They are like cigarette packs. Read the label and apply the information or suffer the possible consequences."

I had a date yesterday, a real date — conversation over soup. He is smart, funny, and accomplished, and we both do yoga. I joked with him about warning labels. Later in the evening, when discussing, with a men's group I facilitate, the pitfalls of dating, I was struck by his warning labels: He was married for years and led a double life, he has not yet told the whole truth of his situation to his 15-year-old son, and his online age is not accurate. There may be good justification for each of these choices, or they could represent a pattern that I know all too well: Facts can be inconvenient in the moment.

I grew up with untruths.

Lou was almost 6 feet tall; he had black hair, graying at the temples, slicked back with Brylcreem, fair skin, light blue eyes, and a big nose that edged between Roman and Sicilian. Although the family was Russian Jewish, the gambling ways and street smarts were pure Mafioso. Big-time Lou was the eldest of Jack and Fannie's seven children, the patron saint, the breadwinner, the guy they all turned to for the answer. To me he was Dad. Although I was his third and last son, I always felt as though my uncles and aunts were his children as well.

You could always find Lou; he was working, or doing something related to sports. It might be watching his older sons' games and meets, or playing the ponies. When I was in junior high, Lou and I began to go to Yonkers Raceway for the trotters, although my mother thought we were bowling. To simulate veracity, we talked about our scores when we got home. On some other plane of reality I became a very good bowler.

Lou thought the truth was necessary only when it was kind. He omitted inconvenient facts and family history. He adjusted circumstance to fit his need.

For example, he changed the cause of his father's death from syphilis to cancer for social acceptance. He seemed to own several businesses, and I never knew what to say about myself when I met his customers, as my mythic self was often a mystery to me and I hated to get him caught out in his lies. A simple factual answer regarding age or accomplishments might reveal one of his stories to be made up. His habit of fabricating reality lasted to the end. After my mother's death, he began secretly dating, but my brothers and I started piecing together the incongruities. He was seeing movies that he would never have seen. He said he played cards on Saturday nights, but card games are never held on a Saturday night in the suburbs. Once he admitted that his girlfriend existed, he tried to keep her from us. Finally one night I dined with dad and PJ. When the check came, I felt his hand under the table thrusting a bill into my hand. I took the cue and paid the check with the proffered C-note without comment, but when we were alone I demanded to know what that was about.

"Well, when we go to dinner with PJ, you always have to pay the check, because I told her that I have no money other than Social Security and that my sons support me — that therefore I could never marry her." That was Lou.

In the course of his long life, he covered up a suicide, protected criminals on the run, and participated in drug running and money laundering ... all the while truly seeing himself as the most upright of citizens. It took some time for me to understand my own relationship to truth. Exaggeration, secrecy, and lies were the very fabric of my childhood, however subtle they usually were. My "a-ha" came when I was about 20, when I realized that getting away with things isn't the greatest challenge; being honest is. Fortunately, I like a challenge.

As I live my life striving for honesty, I have also had to struggle with my childhood tendency to turn a blind eye to the perpetrator of dishonesty, particularly if he is a man I might love.

Is it surprising that I am often attracted to men who might be called "trouble"? This new beau, on the surface, is the upright citizen, the good man I seek, yet there's the pesky issue that his life has been less than transparent. He has a big warning label.

What would you do?

LIVING THE
IMPOSSIBLE DREAM

(Written on my 60th birthday): If I am not grateful, I am truly a fool. When I turned 40, turning 50 seemed unlikely. When I turned 50, I realized that I had no vision for the coming decade. Today I am 60 and I see that the chapters unfold (I just don't get to proofread them ahead of time). I was probably already HIV-positive when I turned 30. Therefore, being here is just wild and amazing and cool and something to wrap my mind around.

However, chapters end. My dear friend Lois Bianchi died last week. She had lived with a chronic and incurable lung ailment for decades, all the while teaching at the university level here and in Croatia as a Fulbright scholar. Only two years ago she went on safari in Africa. She sold stock to do it and didn't tell her family she was going for fear they might try to stop her. She was unreasonable. She was stubborn. She was a warrior!

When I first met Lois, in 1980, we were working for the avant-garde theater director and visionary Robert Wilson. For me, back then, a woman in her 40s was more a mentor than a peer (and Lois was an extraordinary mentor to students and colleagues alike), but as the years went on, Lois, in her generosity of spirit, welcomed my maturation into a comrade — someone who could also support her on her journey. Along the way, we traveled to Tuscany, Baja, and the Vineyard. We lost parents and handled our illnesses. In the end, I had the intimate honor to arrive at her deathbed, along with two dear mutual friends, only moments after she quietly passed on. Lois's spirit lives. Some friends have a hold on our hearts that is eternal.

And here I am, alive. In the 1990s, I was the "designated die-er" in my circle. Only after I rebounded into the previously unknown territory of recovery from AIDS did I see how my family and friends had been understandably organized around the idea that I would be the next one to go. This is a phenomenon that I have come to identify and bust when I see it. Numerous times the seemingly healthy partner or caregiver dies suddenly, due to an undiagnosed illness, an accident, an overdose.... The possibility that we ever know who is leaving next is absurd. All the more reason to make sure that our relationships are up to date and things are not left unsaid. What is better than knowing that your last words to a beloved were "I love you." That was my grace with Lois.

And chapters continue. My work at Friends in Deed as a counselor and group facilitator fulfills me. I am traveling to Turkey and Greece in June to sail the coast on a chartered gulet (a hybrid between a traditional Turkish working boat and a wooden yacht) for the second time, and in December I will return to South Africa in order to deepen my relationship with that continent. I continue to practice AntiGravity Yoga and go to the gym and take my meds and to create a present with a very possible future.

New chapters begin. I've published a book, and in my personal life, I am continuing to explore an intimate relationship with another man by meeting and reacquainting myself with wonderful men of varying ages and backgrounds.

Once again, my life is filled with love and great fortune. My 60s opened up with optimism and with the realistic expectation of challenges and opportunities to come. At this point, I should have little fear — if I've handled the last six decades, I can handle whatever is coming ... Luck and Love!

WHAT IS PATRIOTISM?

A few years ago I counseled a lovely woman who came to Friends In Deed after her 15-year-old son was shot to death while going to the deli for milk. He was not the intended target of the bullet.

During our sessions, this brokenhearted mother asked me for my opinion on a troubling dilemma, "My friends and family say that I should hate the boy who shot my son. Is there something wrong with me? I don't feel hate, only sadness — for my son, for us, for that boy. Am I wrong?"

The response came from my own heart: "Your forgiveness is grace."

During the Truth and Reconciliation process in South Africa, forgiveness trumped revenge. South Africa made the transition from oppressive, white minority rule to inclusive black majority rule without significant violence. That is grace on a huge scale. It is possible.

My aunt was murdered in 1985. I saw the World Trade towers fall from my lower Manhattan building. Tragic events are difficult to integrate into everyday life. As a character in the play *Rabbit Hole* says about the death of a son years earlier: "It was a boulder on my shoulders; now it is a brick in my pocket." We can go on, and forgiveness is crucial. Not that what has occurred is okay, but that it is put down. I have left the largest part of my grief in the past. The brick in my pocket is enough.

Therefore, I am not dancing in the streets because Bin Laden is dead. I am sad. I am moved to remember the Americans who died on September 11, and I am also moved to remember the hundreds of thousands of Afghanis and Iraqis who have died or been left homeless and displaced in the aftermath, not to mention our own killed and wounded soldiers. I mark this occasion with solemn reflection.

I am grateful that our President has behaved with restraint and dignity.

The media images of thrilled, jubilant crowds, in my opinion, are more likely to cause a backlash of terrorism than cow our enemies. Religious and patriotic fundamentalists propagate more violence with an eye-for-an-eye, a never ending cycle of destruction.

This week, several clients came to me fearing that their unease with the celebratory images would make their patriotism suspect. How limited we are if compassion, even-handedness and taking responsibility for our part in things could be seen as un-American. If we are to reclaim our good-guy image on the international scene, we must present a new 21st century model for strength: Honesty, integrity, compassion, willingness to correct for error, to make amends and to be sad at the loss of human life — all human life.

THE SIMPLICITY OF CRISIS

In the abstract, history can be fascinating. When you have lived the history, experience's emotional layers can act as blinders, obscuring the larger picture; relative objectivity is a challenge.

Thirty years ago the first article on AIDS appeared in *The New York Times*. As is often the case, we didn't know in the moment that our lives would never be the same.

The brilliant revival of *The Normal Heart* on Broadway brings it back as a flood of memory and feeling. The gay community was caught up by a tsunami of fear, conjecture, and uncertainty. By the mid '80s, sudden deaths and struggle were commonplace. I remember sipping from the same cup of coffee as my GMHC buddy, his body weakened by Karposi's sarcoma, and thinking, I may have just killed myself. All bodily fluids were still suspect (HIV, carried by blood, had not been identified at that point). Yet I didn't refuse the proffered cup. I didn't want him to be an object of fear.

In tandem with the suffering, we were also experiencing extraordinary beauty. A community came together — those in the first wave, young gay men, were embraced by their brothers (and sisters). We found our soul. If liberation had inadvertently led us to a plague, we could bond together lovingly and effectively. I also remember this as a time of faith and celebration of life.

Crisis is always an opportunity to recalibrate our priorities. At the "front" in wartime, each moment is revealed in its value and clarity without the illusion that it comes with a guaranteed future. I know that those years broke my heart, but I also knew them as a time of wakefulness. I was not on my way to my life, I was in it. Time and again, I have observed that during crisis, life is oddly simple. One must do the next thing, then the next thing, then the next.

In the '90s, when I was critically ill, taking my next breath was my job. Accepting the kindness and practical support of family and friends was easy — I could no longer "earn" their love, it was simply present.

On a personal level, I have no regrets about this part of my journey. I wouldn't be who I am today without all of it — the loss, the not-knowingness, the aliveness that came from savoring the very day, accepting that some of us might not be here tomorrow.

Last night I was talking with a friend in his 20s and I was reminded of the ultimate gift: the realization that just being here to tell him the tale is enough. Being alive is the magic.

That place of simplicity can become obscured but is never fully forgotten. The grace is in remembering it without the need for yet another crisis.

OUTING MR. HYDE

There are photographs of me, many of them by the artist Peter Hujar, another by Robert Mapplethorpe, that could be considered compromising. But I'm proud of them. At 60, I accept my sensual self, past and present.

When a friend, Linda Durham, a respected art dealer and gallery owner in Santa Fe, ran for mayor a number of years ago, she began her campaign by "outing" her past. "As some of you know," she said, "I was at one time a Playboy bunny. That is not relevant to this election. I have been a businesswoman for over twenty years, a mother, an activist in our community. That is what is relevant." It was never mentioned again.

If you can't confront your shadow, it'll bite you in the ass.

We all have a shadow—a dark, often disowned Mr. Hyde. It can fuel creativity and sexual energy. Perhaps it's part of our hardwiring; necessary to spread our seed. But this id, this unconscious mind, can often override our sensible self. Such is the case with Weiner and Schwarzenegger. The subliminal self wants to be caught, to be free from the pretense of one-dimensional "goodness." To pretend to be a symbol of near-perfection is a temptation to the shadow self to act up and out.

Our society expects public figures to behave a certain way. We ask them to only be in their "light," not only to be honest but also traditionally monogamous in their relationships, as if this is part of the job description. Blame our Puritanical culture for this personality split.

Underlying this phenomenon is the classical Madonna/whore dichotomy. For some, the woman they marry becomes the "mother of their children" and can no longer be the object of their lust. Hence a "whore" or "slut" is needed to fill the place of their beloved who is now the virtuous "Madonna."

Some of us don't need that heat in our sex lives. Those of us who do have a challenge: We must transcend the culture's limitations and dare to be shameless with those we love.

My friend Felicity used to call herself a "lady in the drawing room and a whore in the bedroom." A healthy marriage (straight or gay) requires the integration of both the angel and the devil if it is to remain, well, hot. When that's accomplished, the temptations of Internet hook-ups and Twitter "sexting" are mitigated if not eliminated. The shadow has no need to rebel.

I'm all for giving the shadow air and space and treating it with compassion. We are still a young culture and we are grappling with a split between our human reality and an unattainable sacred ideal.

Monogamy is, to be blunt, really difficult. We can begin by concentrating on honest expression of self — monogamous or polyamorous — giving recognition to that shadow, allowing it to be part of the relationship. Marriage can be based on commitment even without the insistence on monogamy as its platform. Women are no longer property and paternity is discernable without chastity belts, figurative or literal.

The media plays its role in either maintaining the status quo or helping us move forward. As long as public figures—and now, with social media, private citizens—are blackmailed by potential exposure of their sexual behavior, the shadow remains underground and a destructive force. When we come out of yet another closet and embrace our full sexual history as inherently valuable, we are free.

Let's give ourselves and our public figures a break and refocus on the greater issues that confront our wellbeing and survival as citizens of the world. Sex scandals are a sideshow to distract us from the real issues: The environment, the economy, human rights!

Photo by R. Levithan

ON DATING SOMEONE YOUNG ENOUGH TO BE YOUR GRANDSON

I'm riding my Segway home from a movie at 11 pm on a Monday night. I stop at the light on Broadway and Prince Street, and a handsome young man walks up to me and says, "Do you realize how cool you are? I've always wanted to ride one of those."

"Hop on," I respond, and he does.

After a spin around Soho, I drop him back at the subway, and we exchange cell numbers. By the next evening, I'm meeting him in Union Square for a date. We're on the Segway again. As I talk about my recent 60th birthday celebrations, I ask him how old he is.

"21."

I almost crash. This is the first time I've been on a date with a man who could be my grandson.

I have a problem that many would not, on the surface, see as a problem: I'm getting hit on by men in their early twenties — a lot.

He reminded me of myself when I was younger. I, too, enjoyed the company of older men; my contemporaries often bored me. He seemed to be an old soul, but by our fifth date, the kid with father/authority issues took over, and it wasn't all fun. We slowed down, changed course and worked it out. We remain in touch—at a distance.

Recently, it was a 25-year-old I met on Grindr. Then there's this 24-year-old who's returning from Turkey next week. I usually think they're older. The Turk has a full beard and is very much an "I'm in charge" kind of guy. That appeals to me. In most of my life, I'm the man in front of the room, the leader; so in romance, I like to relax. However, I can't cede power to a clueless kid. So, what am I getting myself into?

I understand the seduction of it; the charm, the brightness, the excitement of skin that still fits. The parent in me, the avuncular mentor, is also activated. It's not just physical. It feels good to be appreciated for my life experience while also being seen as hot.

Being a Hot Daddy brings all kinds of warning labels and limitations. Is this a subtle (or not so subtle) form of self-sabotage? A new version of pursuing the unavailable man? Getting involved with a man ten or twenty years younger doesn't phase me; thirty-plus years younger feels like too much.

Therefore, I make sure to also date men closer to my own age. I had a date with a 69-year-old recently, and he was truly hot. (Unfortunately, he lives in California.) I'm eager to be non-ageist here and take each man on a one-to-one basis. I counsel clients to not live in policies, to be in the present and examine the actual situation, to look at the individual in front of them and ask, "What's the best relationship I can have with this person?" I wonder, however, if some policies simplify and facilitate rather than merely limit. The statement "I don't date men under 40!" sounds rigid but also oddly liberating. I've made a date for this weekend with a 45-year-old. I have a date next week with the young Turk upon his return. For the moment, I'm holding the contradictions. We'll see where it leads me. I'm playing a very broad field at 60 and proceeding with caution.

RENT REDUX

"Will I lose my dignity? Will someone care? Will I wake tomorrow from this nightmare?"

The moment those lines are sung in *RENT*, I am back there, back in time when we had no idea how we were going to get through it all. Every character in *RENT* who has HIV/AIDS is expecting to die within a few years at most, perhaps in months or weeks.

A few nights ago, I attended the opening night of the new off-Broadway revival of *RENT*. When its original production opened in 1996, I was a few months into anti-viral treatment for AIDS, eighteen months away from nearly dying of AIDS-related Pneumonia. When I was recovering at my home in Santa Fe from that health crisis, my father's dear friend Al Larson came up to visit from Albuquerque, where he lived in retirement. I remember the look of pain on his face. It was very hard for him to see his friend's son so clearly ill, perhaps dying.

Although my life-expectancy then was only a couple of years, I did recover from that opportunistic infection, moved back to New

York City, won a lottery for early access to the first workable "cocktail," and therefore, when Jonathan Larson, the composer and author of *RENT*, Al's son, died suddenly at 35 from an undiagnosed aneurism, just days before the first production of his show opened, it was my father who comforted his friend on the loss of a son.

Now, sixteen years later, Al and I are both still here. When we meet again after the play, as we have several times over the years, I see joy in my apparent (and actual) good health, and a bittersweet pang. How did this happen? Jonathan: so long dead. Me: very much alive. Ironic?

I was the designated die-er in my extended family. We often think we know who is going next; our minds organize around expected outcomes. But again and again, as with Jonathan and me, we are proved wrong. Who dies when is part of the ultimate mystery.

My brilliant niece was also at the opening. (One of *RENT*'s producers is one of her clients.) She was 16 when she first saw a preview of the play. Since then, she has grown up and built a full and rich life that brings me such joy to observe and share. She witnessed my illness and Jonathan's death. A few years ago, she was my date for *RENT*'s 10th-anniversary gala. That night we were stunned to feel the passage of that decade. She was now also an adult, and we were sharing something extraordinary, but it was also something that was once impossible to believe. We do not take this good fortune for granted. We know that it could have been a different path and that through a combination of luck, love, and, yes, perhaps karma, I and many others are here.

For me, the party after the off-Broadway opening was a "This is your life, Robert Levithan" snapshot of the last fifteen years. The circles and layers can come together: the Larsons, my niece, Cynthia O'Neal (the founder of Friends In Deed, the crisis center I work with and upon which the Life Support group in the show is based), clients, performers and friends. We're all connected through this masterwork of exquisite pain and beauty. The privilege of being part of this rich community—the privilege of being alive!

WHEN MONOGAMY IS A COP OUT

Monogamy remains the societal ideal for relationships. Those who choose other forms are pathologized as immature, irresponsible—even defective.

When my relationship with my Brazilian boyfriend was floundering, I stopped and asked myself that important question, "What is the best relationship I can have with this man?" What if I throw out the frame for an "ideal" relationship and strive for one that reflects our actual selves and needs. We were not meant to be monogamous; we weren't meant to live together. We were meant to be friends for life — friends with benefits in that case. I applied this formula to my more recent five-year relationship. We were truly committed lovers. We never pretended exclusivity; we always told the truth and acted with respect.

A recent piece on Dan Savage in *The New York Times* magazine, where he questioned monogamy as the only viable model, was a big deal. It crossed over into the "straight" world with an issue that is always up for discussion amongst gay men. Suddenly my (happily) long-married female friends were talking about the importance of commitment and continuity as primary values, monogamy as secondary, both for couples but also for the family unit.

I know men, straight and gay, who are monogamous by nature. I believe they are the minority. It is a cliché, but males are programmed to reproduce. It's natural to want to get it around. The chemicals released during sex make the male want to linger with the female for an hour or two. The same chemicals released in females last for days, often bringing on the urge to make a nest for the child that might have just been conceived. Our free will, and variances in personality, psyche, chemistry, and environment, creates a spectrum of possibilities for the modern man and woman, but nature significantly influences most of us.

Monogamy as deprivation rarely works. "I will give up what I want in order to have you (and society's blessing)," is the basic idea. Monogamy is valuable as a choice. Opt to be with only one partner in order to explore the depths of that relationship. Every relationship form has its inherent challenges and concomitant rewards. Each of us needs to look at what we are up to and ready for. What matters is commitment to self, partner, the relationship, and the lessons.

A healthy relationship has three members: Two I's and a We. They all need attention and nurturance. For some, monogamy may be necessary to nurture a fragile We. For others, it might starve one or more of the I's.

Ultimately, what matters for a couple (and for the family unit, if they have children) is trust, continuity, and integrity. The first definition of integrity in the dictionary is *wholeness*. What makes us whole? What makes our marriage whole? What makes our family whole? These are questions for which there are so many answers.

Each of us is responsible for identifying our deal breakers. Monogamy can be one, which is fine, as long as it isn't a cop out; an unwillingness to look at what we need, value, and truly hold dear. My honest open relationships have resulted in ongoing intimate friendships with my lovers. Success was in not playing by someone else's rules.

BRAGGING RIGHTS

"Your time is limited, so don't waste it living someone else's life"
~Steve Jobs

Our primary mission on planet earth is the care of our own soul.
This will look different for each of us, of course, and people will
have their opinions about how we choose to do it.

I am not living the life I was brought up to live. This is fortunate as
that life would not suit my emotional and spiritual well-being. This
is not a judgment on other lifestyles —the life we were brought up
to live does suit my oldest brother perfectly, for example.

I have lived my life feeling like an "outsider." It took me a while to
realize that I am gay, but that is not the sum total of my identity. I
came of age in the '60s, and I embraced the revolutionary spirit of
the times: Question everything!

Apple's motto, "Think Different" (even if it is grammatically incor-
rect) speaks to the ongoing challenge to not accept blindly the

values of family, community, or society. Each of us will be tested, perhaps often.

It is simper to accept dogma, party beliefs, and social norms. Simple but uninteresting. What I set out to do when I was younger was to live an interesting life.

Recently, my voice as a writer has been questioned. I was told I could be more discrete in content and tone. Those making the suggestions love me. Like good parents, they want what is best for me, and they fear that I am off key.

My parents discouraged me from being an artist. They discouraged me from living abroad. And, when I became an artist and traveled the world and created a life that was meaningful to me (which, by the way, includes it being hopefully of service to others as well), they embraced it and me. They truly wanted what was best for me, they just couldn't see beyond their own limits.

I believe my friends and colleagues who are worried about me now are coming from a similar place.

I have been accused of bragging, of flaunting my sexuality and physical attributes — my privileges. I have made a choice, knowing that many would see me as a braggart, to neither inflate nor deflate my experience to match the comfort levels of others. Oddly, this is considered edgy.

Humility is a virtue. It is damaging to pretend to be more than we are. However, it is also damaging to pretend to be less than we are. To not share one's successes and triumphs is as inaccurate as hiding one's struggles and disappointments. I don't believe in failure since every situation and experience is another opportunity for growth — sometimes another fucking opportunity for growth, but still worth it!

I began to write The New 60 to counteract the internalized age-ism that causes many young people to fear getting older and many older adults to see themselves as less than vital and powerful. I feel complete with that part of my mission. Now I will continue to write about the even more subtle challenges that I see facing us as we each strive to realize our personal best, regardless of the opinions of others well-intentioned though they might be.

Photo by C. Harrison

60: WHAT'S THE BIG DEAL?

I share my birth date with my friend Joel Grey. On our birthday, April 11th, "Joel Grey's New York," an exhibit of his brilliant photographs of our beloved city, opened at the Museum of the City of New York. He is currently starring in a revival of *Anything Goes*, and directing a production of Larry Kramer's *The Normal Heart* that will also open on Broadway this month. Not bad for a guy who's 79!

Now that I am actually 60, I'm no longer afraid of being 60. I celebrated for a week: lunch, brunch, dinner, theatre, sex, work, a party for ninety people, more lunch, dinner. I'd been writing about this milestone for a full year. I'd been thinking about it for far longer.

I woke up the day after and felt that, oh, right, turning 60 isn't a big deal. The meaning of the number was an idea, a story I'd been told and bought into. I was telling myself that this birthday would matter, that I'd be changed irrevocably.

No. I'm just a day older—and I can no longer die "tragically young."

I remain grateful for having been on the planet for 60 years, for the perspective that comes from living history, not just studying it as I did at college. But Joel's life reminds me that I might just have another chapter or two ahead. What's next?

One section of Joel's exhibit is a wall-size timeline of his career. He's had quite a ride: nightclubs, theater, movies, TV, concerts, experimental theatre, and photography —picking up an Oscar, a Tony, and an Emmy along the way. Joel is one of my inspirations. He exemplifies the wisdom of happiness: Appreciate the past, and be truly engaged in the present.

Aging with grace means finding what one is doing now the most interesting thing in one's already interesting life. I have had some pretty heady experiences as a performer, a teacher, a shrink, and now as a writer. My history is a platform, yet I am most excited about my current projects: writing this book, continuing to work face-to-face with clients, looking for the next space to buy and design, discovering my next relationship, and exploring, as of yet, unrealized ambitions.

Even though I have already accomplished my number one goal, to have an interesting life with some meaning to myself and, I hope, to others, I am certainly not writing my obit. I am summing up six decades as I roll up my sleeves and revel in the great fortune of entering my seventh decade in good health, engaged and curious about what is coming and how I can meet it in the most creative way.

Author Photo by Karen Fuchs

Robert Levithan was born in 1951 on the island of Manhattan. He is a committed New Yorker although time spent in Italy, Venezuela, Brazil and Santa Fe have contributed to his well being. Presently a psychotherapist in private practice in New York City, he also facilitates groups at Friends In Deed—The Crisis Center for Life Threatening Illness—where he was Co-Chair of the Board for seven years. He also leads the Mastery Workshop. He is a columnist for *The Good Men Project Magazine* and a frequent contributor to *The Huffington Post*. His rather varied past experiences include dancing for Twyla Tharp, performing with Robert Wilson and under the direction of Roman Polanski and driving a NYC Taxi. He co-produced the first productions of *The Vagina Monologues, One Man Band and Word of Mouth*, the source of *Trevor,* the Academy award winning film that led to the creation of the Trevor Project-the suicide hotline for LGBT teens. He has written columns for *OPRAH at HOME* as The Design Shrink and for OUT.com and ADVOCATE.com. As an expert on living with illness, he has appeared on CHARLIE ROSE and FRESH AIR and is cited in numerous books and articles. He currently lives in SoHo with his muse, Sophie, a former seeing-eye dog. He is working on a memoir.

Made in the USA
Charleston, SC
17 April 2012